DJ, Dance, and Rave Culture

EXAMINING POP CULTURE

JARED F. GREEN, Book Editor

Bruce Glassman, Vice President
Bonnie Szumski, Publisher
Helen Cothran, Managing Editor

GREENHAVEN PRESS
An imprint of Thomson Gale, a part of The Thomson Corporation

THOMSON
─────✱─────™
GALE

Detroit • New York • San Francisco • San Diego • New Haven, Conn.
Waterville, Maine • London • Munich

© 2005 Thomson Gale, a part of The Thomson Corporation.

Thomson and Star Logo are trademarks and Gale and Greenhaven Press are registered trademarks used herein under license.

For more information, contact
Greenhaven Press
27500 Drake Rd.
Farmington Hills, MI 48331-3535
Or you can visit our Internet site at http://www.gale.com

ALL RIGHTS RESERVED.
No part of this work covered by the copyright hereon may be reproduced or used in any form or by any means—graphic, electronic, or mechanical, including photocopying, recording, taping, Web distribution or information storage retrieval systems—without the written permission of the publisher.

Every effort has been made to trace the owners of copyrighted material.

Cover credit: © Brand X Pictures

LIBRARY OF CONGRESS CATALOGING-IN-PUBLICATION DATA

DJ, dance, and rave culture / Jared F. Green, book editor.
   p. cm.—(Examining pop culture series)
  Includes bibliographical references and index.
  ISBN 0-7377-2547-8 (lib. : alk. paper)
    1. Techno music—History and criticism. 2. Rave culture. I. Green, Jared F.
  II. Series.
  ML3540.D4 2005
  781.64—dc22   2004059791

Printed in the United States of America

CONTENTS

both musician and integral part of the dance club experience.

Chapter 3: Dancing into the New Millennium

POPULAR CULTURE IS THE COMMON SET OF ARTS, entertainments, customs, beliefs, and values shared by large segments of society. Russel B. Nye, one of the founders of the study of popular culture, wrote that "not until the appearance of mass society in the eighteenth century could popular culture, as one now uses the term, be said to exist." According to Nye, the Industrial Revolution and the rise of democracy in the eighteenth and nineteenth centuries led to increased urbanization and the emergence of a powerful middle class. In nineteenth-century Europe and North America, these trends created audiences for the popular arts that were larger, more concentrated, and more well off than at any point in history. As a result, more people shared a common culture than ever before.

The technological advancements of the twentieth century vastly accelerated the spread of popular culture. With each new advance in mass communication—motion pictures, radio, television, and the Internet—popular culture has become an increasingly pervasive aspect of everyday life.

Popular entertainment—in the form of movies, television, theater, music recordings and concerts, books, magazines, sporting events, video games, restaurants, casinos, theme parks, and other attractions—is one very recognizable aspect of popular culture. In his 1999 book *The Entertainment Economy: How Mega-Media Forces Are Transforming Our Lives*, Michael J. Wolf argues that entertainment is becoming the dominant feature of American society: "In choosing where we buy French fries, how we relate to political candidates, what airline we want to fly, what pajamas we choose for our kids, and which mall we want to buy them in, entertainment is increasingly influencing every one of those choices. . . . Multiply that by the billions of choices that, collectively, all of us make each day and you have a portrait of a society in which entertainment is one of its leading institutions."

It is partly this pervasive quality of popular culture that makes it worthy of study. James Combs, the author of *Polpop: Politics and Popular Culture in America*, explains that examining

popular culture is important because it can shape people's attitudes and beliefs:

> Popular culture is so much a part of our lives that we cannot deny its developmental powers. . . . Like formal education or family rearing, popular culture is part of our "learning environment.". . . Though our pop culture education is informal—we usually do not attend to pop culture for its "educational" value—it nevertheless provides us with information and images upon which we develop our opinions and attitudes. We would not be what we are, nor would our society be quite the same, without the impact of popular culture.

Examining popular culture is also important because popular movies, music, fads, and the like often reflect popular opinions and attitudes. Christopher D. Geist and Jack Nachbar explain in *The Popular Culture Reader*, "the popular arts provide a gauge by which we can learn what Americans are thinking, their fears, fantasies, dreams, and dominant mythologies. The popular arts reflect the values of the multitude."

This two-way relationship between popular culture and society is evident in many modern discussions of popular culture. Does the glorification of guns by many rap artists, for example, merely reflect the realities of inner-city life, or does it also contribute to the problem of gun violence? Such questions also arise in discussions of the popular culture of the past. Did the Vietnam protest music of the late 1960s and early 1970s, for instance, simply reflect popular antiwar sentiments, or did it help turn public opinion against the war? Examining such questions is an important part of understanding history.

Greenhaven Press's *Examining Pop Culture* series provides students with the resources to begin exploring these questions. Each volume in the series focuses on a particular aspect of popular culture, with topics as varied as popular culture itself. Books in the series may focus on a particular genre, such as *Rap and Hip Hop*, while others may cover a specific medium, such as *Computers and the Internet*. Volumes such as *Body Piercing and Tattoos* have their focus on recent trends in popular culture, while titles like *Americans' Views About War* have a broader historical scope.

In each volume, an introductory essay provides a general

overview of the topic. The selections that follow offer a survey of critical thought about the subject. The readings in *Americans' Views About War*, for example, are arranged chronologically: Essays explore how popular films, songs, television programs, and even comic books both reflected and shaped public opinion about American wars from World War I through Vietnam. The essays in *Violence in Film and Television*, on the other hand, take a more varied approach: Some provide historical background, while others examine specific genres of violent film, such as horror, and still others discuss the current controversy surrounding the issue.

Each book in the series contains a comprehensive index to help readers quickly locate material of interest. Perhaps most importantly, each volume has an annotated bibliography to aid interested students in conducting further research on the topic. In today's culture, what is "popular" changes rapidly from year to year and even month to month. Those who study popular culture must constantly struggle to keep up. The volumes in Greenhaven's *Examining Pop Culture* series are intended to introduce readers to the major themes and issues associated with each topic, so they can begin examining for themselves what impact popular culture has on their own lives.

AMERICAN RAVE BEGAN ON A MODEST SCALE, when about eighty people, drawn together by word of mouth, gathered on Baker Beach in San Francisco to dance to throbbing electronic music on a moonlit March evening in 1991. In something of a feedback loop, the idea of staging an illegal dance gathering had migrated from England, where American techno and house music from Detroit and Chicago had ignited the UK rave revolution in the late 1980s. In 1992, when the California "Full Moon Raves" celebrated the first anniversary of their monthly gatherings, over one thousand people showed up to dance on a Santa Cruz beach. Two years later the crowd swelled to three thousand, and rave was no longer just a rumor. By the year 2000 rave was being hailed by some as a rising form of global cultural expression even as others were already mourning its death.

In examining the rave phenomenon, it becomes clear that the answer to the question of whether rave is alive or dead depends on one's definition of rave. If one defines rave as a unique countercultural or subcultural movement, it could be argued that rave never really existed. If such a culture ever did truly exist, rave's growing popularity has led to a loss of the outlaw elusiveness and fringe status that were considered to be the very essence of rave. Nevertheless, it is more useful to think of rave not as a subculture but as an attitude—a spirit of youthful, pleasure-driven, anticorporate communal idealism set to the rhythms and beats of DJ-produced electronic music. Indeed, these aspects of the rave scene of the 1990s—electronic music, the role of the DJ, and a spirit of communal solidarity—are alive and well in newer forms of dance culture.

A Celebration of Freedom

In its strictest sense rave can be defined as a dance gathering that, unlike club dancing, takes place outside of the legal parameters that govern such activities. Often staged in illegally accessed warehouses and industrial spaces or even in rural expanses, raves have always had an aura of countercultural force,

guerrilla activity, trespass, and transgression. Accordingly, one cannot properly speak of raves without acknowledging the role of illegal hallucinogenic and stimulant drugs, especially MDMA (ecstasy), which has become practically synonymous with the rave experience. Defenders of rave culture often minimize the prominence of drugs and emphasize instead a tribalistic or quasi-spiritual collectivity as the meaning of rave. For example, in *Rave Culture: An Insider's Overview*, author Jimi Fritz quotes a rave promoter and DJ from Japan whose account of his rave experiences emphasizes both the spirituality of dance and rave's ability to provide a liberatory social space outside of the norms of a restrictive mainstream culture: "Rave culture has changed my whole life. I was brought up in Tokyo in a middle class family and had no appreciation for nature or connections to other people. Rave culture and trance music has given me direction and spiritual fulfillment. My life is more valuable to me now. I have seen other people change too. They become happier."[1] While this may indeed be the case for some ravers—Fritz quotes one Finnish raver who extols rave as simply a "modern high-tech form of an ancient tribal ritual where shamans gather to dance themselves into deep trance or self-hypnosis"[2]—it remains true that drugs are integral to rave culture and largely responsible for its eroticized atmosphere and psychedelic aesthetic.

To be sure, the proliferation of illegal drugs and the potential dangers for those who consume them cannot be overlooked, but drugs are only one aspect of the overall culture of rave and dance and should not be confused with the more fundamental freedom celebrated by the electronic music that is rave's raison d'être. Although rave's public image is irrevocably associated with ecstasy consumption, it would be an error to reduce the meaning of rave to its associated intoxicants. In counterpoint to this common misperception, internationally renowned DJ Paul Oakenfold insists that the feeling of transport—that is, of being moved beyond the boundaries of the body and of everyday consciousness—is intrinsic to the music itself: "The qualities in this music that effect people so deeply are the energy and the melody. It's uplifting and spiritual. There's a lot of soul in it and it really is about the feeling. It's similar to soul music in that you listen to it from an emotional

standpoint."[3] The feeling to which Oakenfold eludes is more than just the joy of the individual dancer as he or she becomes lost in the music; it is the emotional and social solidarity felt by the dancers joined together—however temporarily—as a new organism created by the music.

But whether drug induced or music induced, in this seductive invitation to suspend social and legal norms and "lose yourself" in the beat, rave was nothing new. The desire for a form of celebration free from the rules that usually regulate everyday life is an impulse as old as civilization itself. As Australian composer David Cox has commented, "[Rave is] the same Dionysian urge [as in ancient Greece], although instead of going into the woods with jugs of wine and lyres and harps, it's technology providing the music and the substances are designer drugs."[4] While rave's inducement to seek pleasure in community (and mind-altering substances) may tap into something universal in human culture, its signature elements, especially the raver creed of PLUR—or "Peace, Love, Unity, Respect"—can be traced to the more recent utopian youth culture that developed around rock music (especially psychedelic rock) in the 1960s. This link did not escape ravers themselves, particularly those in the UK who referred to the nascent rave scene of 1987 as the "second summer of love," a reference to the popular phrase used for the hippie counterculture that emerged in San Francisco in 1967. What was truly unique about rave, then, was not its counterculture posturing, but rather the very things that have outlived rave's initial cultural moment: propulsive electronic music and the prominent position of the DJ as artist and performer.

Rave as Subculture

Despite its association with the 1960s counterculture, the rave phenomenon does not meet the definition of "subculture" in its strictest meaning. In his 1947 essay, "The Concept of the Subculture and Its Application," sociologist Milton Gordon first defined a subculture as a "sub-division of a national culture, composed of a combination of factorable social situations such as class status, ethnic background, regional and rural or urban residence, and religious affiliation, but forming in their combination a functioning unity which has an integrated impact on

the participating individual."[5] Gordon was speaking specifically of ethnic groups within post–World War II American culture, but the overall utility of his definition of "subculture" has found a long afterlife as a means for analyzing youth-culture movements. Despite the frequency with which this term appears in writing on rave, however, there is a problem with its usage, for outside of the basic trappings that distinguish the dance party known as a rave (e.g., the DJ, the illegally accessed space, lights, particular dance styles and fashions, and so on), rave cannot be spoken of as a uniform movement or organized community. Moreover, Gordon's notion of subculture misrepresents rave because it does not account for the diversity of ethnicities, belief systems, sexual orientations, and class affiliations that blend into a temporarily unified social body during the course of a rave event. This cross-cultural unity, indicative of the broad appeal of rave, does not translate to a stable community once the sun rises and the music fades. Unlike actual subcultures, there is no physically defined space (as there is in, say, New York's Chinatown or Paris' Le Marais Jewish quarter) in which people devoted to the rave lifestyle live and work as an identifiable subset within a dominant national culture. When the party ends, ravers return to their neighborhoods, schools, and offices until they find one another again at the next event.

To the extent that rave does constitute a distinct culture, the integrity of that culture has surely been compromised by rave's commercialization. What is most commonly meant by the oft-repeated statement that "rave is dead" is that something of the "authenticity" of those early raves seems to have vanished as rave-style dance events and the electronic music that was the core of rave's being have become more widespread and thus more mainstream. The crux of this argument lies in the observation that rave is founded on a principle of absolute opposition to mainstream pop and consumerism. Considered in such terms, the rave posture of permanent outsidership is impossible to sustain once it reaches widespread acceptance and begins to attract the interest of corporate sponsors, event promoters, and advertising executives. This seemingly unavoidable irony—that the community so important to ravers would be undone by the expansion of this community—is an auto-destruct mechanism built into the logic of all "alternative" or

"edge" cultures and accounts for why rave has been pronounced dead from virtually the moment it was born.

Cultural historian Dick Hebdige usefully notes that this inverse ratio of popularity to "authenticity" can be reliably explained by the fact that, in capitalist societies, popular cultural forms and movements are inevitably subject to the twin forces of what he calls "diffusion" and "defusion."[6] For Hebdige, the two terms are linked in something of a downward spiral, in which "diffusion," or the spread of a subcultural style through mainstream media coverage, inexorably leads to "defusion," or the loss of the symbolic resistance that the original subculture may have had. In Hebdige's Marxist-influenced account of how countercultures are transformed as they enter the mainstream, the key element is not so much that increased popularity imperils the intimate, tribalistic aura of the original movement, but rather that when corporate interests commodify an "alternative" cultural form (as has been the case with jazz, rock, punk, and hip-hop), they evacuate that form of any ability to offer true, sustained resistance to the dominant culture from which it once offered refuge.

Given the undeniable commercialization that has taken hold of both large-scale, rave-style dance gatherings and the music so intimately associated with rave, it seems difficult to argue that anything of the original rave culture could possibly continue to thrive. More appropriate than a strict application of Gordon's term *subculture*, then, is his companion concept of the *sub-cultural personality*. This term refers to a more fluid set of attitudes that find expression in the individual and defines his or her persona (by way of clothing, musical tastes, etc.) in terms of the rave *lifestyle*. Perhaps it is as a subcultural personality—that is, as the *idea* of a way of being that is outside the boundaries of mainstream culture—that rave continues to exert its most powerful influence. Indeed, whatever rave culture was in the 1980s and 1990s, it was only one articulation of a more significant and enduring spirit that must constantly change in order to remain a valid form of youth-culture expression.

The DJ and the Music

As noted above, rave grew out of one generation's dance culture, and what it has bequeathed as its legacy is a transformed,

updated, streamlined, and accelerated dance culture that speaks to a new generation of dancers. What was truly unique about rave culture—the music and the DJs that made and performed it—are the elements that have exceeded rave itself to become vital components of an ever-expanding global youth culture that has thus far proven itself impervious to crass commercialization. In order to see how rave as a collective energy continues to find vital expression in contemporary life, it is necessary to examine the intertwined elements of the DJ and the music as, on the one hand, integral to the rave event and, on the other, worthy of separate consideration.

While the DJ has a distinct social role that clearly depends upon his or her relationship to the dancer, DJs have developed a subcultural personality of their own—one centered primarily on the collection of interesting source music to manipulate, the programming of beats on drum machines, and the organization of music in order to create a rhythmic flow that will keep dancers energized well into the night. As British DJs Bill Brewster and Frank Broughton insist, however, DJs are not simply music collectors and shadowy figures behind the turntables; they have transformed the way that music is made, played, and consumed in the digital age. The role of the DJ in the construction of music and the overall dance experience represents one of the most radical transformations in music composition and performance since the electrification of instruments. This radicalism is especially visible in what is prized by independent and underground DJs as the DIY (do-it-yourself) ethic. In contrast to the more commercialized aspects of DJ culture—and thus still closely allied with the spirit of early rave—DIY describes the approach of those DJs who create music on laptop computers or who generate their own music by pressing homemade (as opposed to prerecorded) beats on acetate or programming them to deploy live on drum machines along with samples collected from throughout the sonic environment.

Sampling, a practice developed first by early electronic music pioneers such as Karlheinz Stockhausen and then transformed into a popular art form by hip-hop DJs, is surely one of the most intriguing and limitless facets of electronic music, as it allows the DJ to assemble compositions from fragments of previously recorded music, giving the sampled excerpt al-

tered meaning in its new context. Closely related to the practice of sampling is that of remixing, the form of musical reinvention that is among the truly unique tactics in the arsenal of the DJ. Simply put, remixing involves taking a previously recorded track and altering aspects of the original song's composition, structure, and instrumentation to reconceptualize the original and take it in new directions. In other words, remixing is a form of collage art that turns recorded music into what computer programmers call the "open source code," available for anyone to see, tinker with, and improve.

The final products that the DJ assembles out of these bits and pieces usually wind up on a DJ mixtape, a highly personalized expression of the independent DJ's art. Electronic music, like hip-hop, has a profusion of independent recording labels and an active underground that circulates these mixtapes. Many of the mixtapes retain an aspect of the anticorporate, outlaw sensibility of the rave, as they gleefully violate copyright laws by taking a previously recorded song in its entirety and recombining it with another song to produce the radical, hybrid form known as a mashup. As music critic Sasha Frere-Jones notes,

> Mashup artists . . . have found a way of bringing pop music to a formal richness that it only rarely reaches. See mashups as piracy if you insist, but it is more useful, viewing them through the lens of the market, to see them as an expression of consumer dissatisfaction. Armed with free time and the right software, people are rifling through the lesser songs of pop music and, in frustration, choosing to make some of them as good as the great ones.[7]

As a response to prefabricated pop and to the idea of a musical composition as the sole possession of its composer, the remix and its cousin, the mashup, are both anarchic and democratic, making any given composition only the first in a potentially endless series of additions, subtractions, and mutations.

Music for a Global Culture

It is this sort of collage aesthetic, the pastiche that commingles the styles, sounds, and voices of past and present, that makes electronic music—above and beyond its connection to the rave

moment of the early 1990s—one of the signal forms of postmodern culture. Indeed, electronic music is one of the rare popular forms that can easily absorb the musical idioms of other cultures. After all, only electronic music can allow a DJ-composer to produce a song in which sitars and tabla drums, bubblegum pop, disco diva vocals, Jamaican dub, balalaikas, and Roland 808s sound seamlessly organic. Given such a uniquely cross-cultural range, it is little wonder that the 2004 summer Olympic Games in Athens, a rare example of a truly global spectacle, were kicked off with a set by Dutch trance superstar DJ Tiesto. Tiesto's fellow superstar DJ, John Digweed, has commented on the growth of electronic music and the dance culture that blossoms in its aura:

> I think the scene will just get bigger. In the last five or six years I've seen it become a huge worldwide scene. I play in countries all over the world and get pretty much the same reaction everywhere I go. I think that in the future we will see more and more people making electronic music in pockets all over the world taking elements from different cultures and just keep growing. The music is truly international.[8]

And this, in the end, is what rave has become: a way of linking through music and dance to the experience of an emerging global consciousness. In a hyperreal, accelerated culture increasingly defined by the eyeblink pace at which digitized sounds, images, and fragments of information flow through the veins and arteries of the global circulatory system, the DJ has at his or her fingertips the ability to spin new forms of music out of the information-saturated ether. These forms can speak to and through the experience of twenty-first-century modernity in all its anger, fear, passion, hope, violence, complexity, and beauty. Both revolution and evolution, the electronic music that fueled early rave has now multiplied and filled the earth. The beat diaspora has circulated its energies to all corners of the globe. If rave is indeed dead, as so many insist, its passing is nothing to lament, for the music that was always the core of its being appears to have found an inexhaustible afterlife as the sound of the worldwide youth culture of dance. But then, rave has long been more a principle of connectivity and expressive freedom rather than a particular type

of social event, and it is this principle that continues to thrive wherever DJs, dancers, and electronic music gather together.

Notes

1. Jimi Fritz, *Rave Culture: An Insider's Overview*. Victoria, BC, Canada: Smallfry, 1999, p. 172.
2. Fritz, *Rave Culture*, p. 187.
3. Quoted in Fritz, *Rave Culture*.
4. Quoted in Chris Zwar, "Rave Culture: Spirituality at 120 Beats per Minute," *St.-Matthew-in-the-City*. www.stmatthews.org.nz/A024.htm.
5. Milton Gordon, "The Concept of the Sub-Culture and Its Application," in *The Subcultures Reader*. Ed. Ken Gelder and Sarah Thornton. London, UK: Routledge, 1997, p. 41.
6. Dick Hebdige, "The Function of Subculture," in *The Cultural Studies Reader*. Ed. Simon During. New York: Routledge, 1999, pp. 441–45.
7. Sasha Frere-Jones, "1+1+1=1: The New Math of Mashups," *New Yorker*, January 10, 2005, pp. 85–86.
8. Quoted in Fritz, *Rave Culture*, p. 266.

CHAPTER

The Origins of Electronic Music

What Is Electronic Music?

Thom Holmes

Thom Holmes, a composer and electronic music performer, demonstrates his firsthand knowledge of the
technologies, techniques, and genres that make electronic music one of the most creative and diverse
forms of avant-garde and popular music. Holmes's
careful explanation of such key terms as *tape music*
and *electroacoustic music* and his clear distinction between analog and digital sound synthesis guide the
reader toward an understanding of the essentials of
electronic music's concepts and practices. In addition
to having a career in musical composition and performance, Holmes is also a software engineer and the
former publisher of *Recordings of Electronic Music*, the
offspring of which, *Electronic Music Magazine*, continues to enjoy a wide circulation today. His book *Electronic and Experimental Music* was originally published
in 1985 and revised and updated in 2002. This excerpt is from the most recent edition.

THE FIELD OF MUSIC IS FULL OF UNINFORMATIVE
labels and categories. Electronic music has not escaped this
phenomenon. During the heyday of institutionalized electronic music in the '50s, even the founders of the music had
difficulty agreeing on what to call it. [Pierre] Schaeffer and
[Pierre] Henry called their combination of synthetic and natural sounds "musique concrète." [Herbert] Eimert and [Karl-
heinz] Stockhausen called their music of purely synthetic ori-

■

Thom Holmes, *Electronic and Experimental Music*. New York: Routledge, 2002. Copyright © 1985 by Thom Holmes. Reproduced by permission of Routledge/Taylor &
Francis Books, Inc., and the author.

gins "elektronische Musik." [Edgard] Varèse called his combination of synthetic and processed natural sounds "organized sound." [Otto] Luening and [Vladimir] Ussachevsky called it "tape-music."

The situation is no less confusing today. Try and explain the differences between ambient, illbient, minimalism, new age, space music, electronica, techno, environmental, avant-garde, downtown (in New York), proto-techno, electro, Krautrock, world, dub, trance, house, acid house, rave, and just plain old electronic music. Most of these so-called genres exist as points on a single continuous spectrum of music that wouldn't be possible without electronics. Trying to define them any further than that is unhelpful.

I decided not to pigeonhole works of electronic music into those kinds of uninformative genres. Instead, it makes more sense to me to discuss the music from the standpoint of composition: the aesthetic and technological approaches used by a composer to work with the sound material. This requires an understanding of the technology that aids the composer, for in the field of electronic music the creative act is securely tethered to the equipment. A discussion of musique concrète must also be a part of a discussion of tape recorders, tape loops, and the kinds of sound manipulation that can take place because of tape editing. Other technology and approaches that drive the nature of a composer's work include process music, turntablism, and tools that can be used for real-time electronic music production in live performance. By discussing the music in this way I hope to acknowledge the unavoidable influence of technology on the composer while at the same time providing a framework within which different approaches to composition can be illuminated. It also allows for the easy grouping of works of similar conceptual and technical origins so that they can be compared and contrasted.

The stuff of electronic music is *electrically produced or modified sounds.* A synthesizer, sine wave generator, and a doorbell all use electrically produced sounds. An amplified violin connected to a wah-wah pedal, or a voice being embellished by electronic reverberation, are examples of ways to modify sounds.

This is perhaps as broad a definition as one can have of electronic music short of admitting that everything we listen

to can be defined in this way. The lines are often blurred between sounds that originate from purely electronic sources and sounds from the real world that are synthetically modified. But I will use two basic definitions that will help put some of the historical discussion in its place: purely electronic music versus electroacoustic music.

Purely Electronic Music

Purely electronic music is created through the generation of sound waves by electrical means. This is done without the use of traditional musical instruments or of sounds found in nature, and is the domain of computers, synthesizers, and other technologies. It is the realm of programs, computer displays, and "virtual" instruments found in software.

Ensembles for Synthesizer (1961–63) by Milton Babbitt (b. 1916) is an example of purely electronic music. It is a twelve-tone piece exploring different "ensembles" of rapidly changing pitches, rhythms, and timbres. It was composed using the RCA Music Synthesizer at the Columbia-Princeton Electronic Music Center. *Switched-On Bach* (1968) by Wendy Carlos (b. 1939) is an example of purely electronic music in which Carlos performs keyboard music of Bach using only the Moog synthesizer.

Purely electronic music can be made through either *analog* or *digital* synthesis. The difference between the two merely lies in the way electricity is controlled. There are no aesthetic differences between the outcomes, and the listener will probably not be able to tell the difference.

In analog synthesis, composers work with continuous electrical current that is *analogous* to its corresponding sound waves. The sound begins as an electric current (alternating current, or AC). The vibrating pattern of the current can be controlled by the composer to create regular or irregular patterns. This current is then fed to an amplifier and loudspeakers, which convert the electrical oscillations into air pressure waves that can be detected by the ear. The resulting sound waves vibrate at the same rate as the electrical waves produced by the electrical sound source. The vibrations of the electric current are controlled by triggering devices such as rotating dials and piano-style keyboards. Analog sounds can be gener-

ated by something as simple as a buzzer or sound-wave oscillator, or by an instrument designed more specifically for musical applications such as an electric guitar or analog synthesizer.

Making sound digitally requires computer circuitry that can generate sound waves. Home computers, toys, digital synthesizers, and video games do this through the use of sound chips. Instead of working directly with the control of continuous electric current, a sound chip represents sound waves as binary information, coded into a series of "on" and "off" electrical pulses. This bitstream represents sounds using the same principles that a computer uses to represent numbers or letters of the alphabet. Different pitches are represented by different codes. Because human hearing is an analog process, digital signals must be converted to analog signals before they can be heard. To make the sound patterns audible, the computer converts the codes into an analog form of electrical current that can be amplified and used to operate a loudspeaker. This is done through what is called a digital-to-analog converter. Once the digital codes are converted into continuous electric current and fed to a speaker system, they sound the same as sounds produced through conventional analog means. The reverse process can be used to get analog sounds into a computer for digitization; they are converted using an analog-to-digital converter and then controlled by the computer.

The benefits of digitally generated sound synthesis are many. Like anything else that can be done on a computer, sounds can be controlled and organized with unprecedented ease, in comparison to the rigors of manipulating analog sounds on tape. Digital sounds can be cut and pasted, modified using special effects, made louder or softer, and structured to precise time measurements. Digital sound has the added benefit of being devoid of hiss and other audio artifacts of analog tape recording. The music that results can be copied directly to an audio CD for listening, storage, and distribution.

The term "synthesis" refers to the process of constructing sounds using electronic, or synthetic, means. The music synthesizer is a device designed to generate purely electronic sounds by analog or digital means. Prior to 1980, most commercially available synthesizers were analog.

Electroacoustic Music

Electroacoustic music uses electronics to modify sounds from the natural world. The entire spectrum of worldly sounds provides the source material for this music. This is the domain of microphones, tape recorders, and digital samplers.

The term "electroacoustic music" can be associated with live or recorded music. During live performance, natural sounds are modified in real time using electronics. The source of the sound can be anything from ambient noise to live musicians playing conventional instruments.

Cartridge Music (1960) by John Cage (1912–1992) is a work of electroacoustic music in which phono cartridges were used to amplify sounds that were otherwise nearly inaudible. *Rainforest IV* (1973) by David Tudor (1926–1996) used the amplified and processed sounds of vibrating objects freely suspended in the performing space. The sounds were amplified, filtered, mixed, and also recycled to make other objects vibrate.

The manipulation of recorded, naturally occurring sounds is the foundation of much electronic music. The classic art of composing electronic music using magnetic tape was not conceptually very different from what is called "digital sampling" today. The objective in each case is to capture sounds from the real world that can then be used, and possibly modified, by the composer.

The amplification of traditional musical instruments is a form of electroacoustic music, but for the purposes of this book such work only crosses the line into the realm of electronic music if the musician uses technology to modify the sound.

The interaction of live musicians playing electronically modified or processed acoustic instruments has been a popular approach with composers. In *Mikrophonie I* (1964) by Karlheinz Stockhausen (b. 1928), the sounds of a tam-tam are picked up by two microphones, amplified, and processed through electronic filters. *Wave Train* (1966) by David Behrman (b. 1937) which threw away all established techniques for playing the piano, consisted of controlled feedback caused by guitar pickups placed on the strings of a piano. *Superior Seven* (1992) by Robert Ashley (b. 1930) used real-time digital processing to extend and embellish the notes played by a flutist.

Using Different Ears

Electronic music exists *because* it is conceived and created with electronic instruments. Does this make it different from other kinds of music? Don't we listen to it with the same set of ears?

[Twentieth-century American composer] Aaron Copland observed that "we all listen to music, professionals and non-professional alike, in the same sort of way—in a dumb sort of way, really, because simple or sophisticated music attracts all of us, in the first instance, on the primordial level of sheer rhythmic and sonic appeal."

As attractive as this observation is, I will argue that we listen to electronic music with different ears, and a different state of mind. One day this will not be the case. Our taste and perceptual constructs will evolve to the point where music of non-acoustic origins will be treated with the same objectivity as all other music, in Copland's "dumb sort of way." But today, hardly fifty years into the recorded medium of electronic music, we have barely been able to get past the technology and think only about the music. Composer-technicians are still most at home in this field. Anyone who composes with synthesizers, software, and computers knows very well that the technology of electronic music has not yet reached the "appliance" stage. When it does, the necessities of *composing* will preoccupy composers instead of the necessities of *mechanics*, the knowledge needed to push the correct buttons and plug in the correct components.

Electronic music is not entirely alien to us. It shares many characteristics with other music. It is emotionally charged and designed to absorb one's attention. Even the most colorless music, stripped of all ornamentation, is fraught with emotional implications. Charles Ives took the twelve-tone composers to task when he wrote, "Is not all music program music? Is not pure music, so called, representative in its essence? Is it not program music raised to the nth power, or, rather, reduced to the minus nth power? Where is the line to be drawn between the expression of subjective and objective emotion?" The listening experience is psychological and fluid, moving forward incessantly, demanding that we take notice or miss out.

Seven Reasons Why Electronic Music Is Different

The sound resources available to electronic music are unlimited and can be constructed from scratch. One of the key differences between electronic music and music composed for traditional instruments is that *its sonic vistas are limitless and undefined.* The composer not only creates the music, but *composes* the very sounds themselves. Herbert Eimert (1897–1972), one of the founders of the Studio für Elektronische Musik [The Studio for Electronic Music] in Cologne, expressed the innate potential of electronic music this way:

> The composer, in view of the fact that he is no longer operating within a strictly ordained tonal system, finds himself confronting a completely new situation. He sees himself commanding a realm of sound in which the musical material appears for the first time as a malleable continuum of every known and unknown, every conceivable and possible sound. This demands a way of thinking in new dimensions, a kind of mental adjustment to the thinking proper to the materials of electronic sound.

Any imaginable sound is fair game. The composer can invent sounds that do not exist in nature or radically transform natural sounds into new instruments. For *Thema–Omaggio a Joyce* (1958), Luciano Berio (b. 1925) used tape manipulation to transform the spoken voice into a myriad of sound patterns eerily laced with the tonalities of human communication. In the piece *Luna* (from *Digital Moonscapes*, 1984), Wendy Carlos modeled a digital instrument whose voice could be modified in real time as it played a theme, metamorphosing from the sound of a violin to a clarinet to a trumpet and ending with a cello sound. This sound wasn't possible in the world outside of the computer, but became possible with her library of "real-world orchestral replicas" that the GDS and Synergy synthesizers allowed. For *Beauty in the Beast* (1986), she took this experimentation a step further by [as she stated] "designing instrumental timbres that can't exist at all, extrapolated from the ones that do exist."

Electronic music expands our perception of tonality. The ac-

26

cepted palette of musical sounds was extended in two directions. On one hand, the invention of new pitch systems became easier with electronic musical instruments. Microtonal music is more easily engineered by a composer who can subdivide an octave using software and a digital music keyboard than by a piano builder. On the other hand, electronic music stretched the concept of pitch in the opposite direction, toward less and less tonality and into the realm of noise. All sounds became equal, just another increment on the electromagnetic spectrum. Varèse sensed this early on and introduced controlled instances of noise in his instrumental and electronic music. Cage accepted the value of all sounds without question and let them be themselves:

> Noises are as useful to new music as so-called musical tones, for the simple reason that they are sounds. This decision alters the view of history, so that one is no longer concerned with tonality or atonality, Schoenberg or Stravinsky (the twelve tones or the twelve expressed as seven plus five), nor with consonance and dissonance, but rather with Edgard Varèse (1885–1965) who fathered forth noise into twentieth-century music. But it is clear that ways must be discovered that allow noises and tones to be just noises and tones, not exponents subservient to Varèse's imagination.

Electronic music only exists in a state of actualization. [Russian-born modernist composer] Igor Stravinsky (1882–1971) wrote that "it is necessary to distinguish two moments, or rather two states of music: potential music and actual music. . . . It exists as a *score*, unrealized, and as a *performance.*" You will rarely find an electronic work that can be accurately transcribed and reproduced from sheet music. It does not exist as "potential music" except in the form of notes, instructions, and ideas made by the composer. Conventional musical notation is not practical for electronic music. You cannot study it as you would a piece of scored music. Experiencing electronic music is, by its nature, a part of its actualization. The term "realization" was aptly adopted by electronic music pioneers to describe the act of assembling a finished work. Even those works that are transcriptions of conventionally composed chromatic music cannot be fully described on paper, because the elements of electronic

instrumentation, sound processing, and performance defy standardization. A work of electronic music is not *real*, does not exist, until a performance is *realized*, or played in real time.

Electronic music has a special relationship with the temporal nature of music. [According to Stravinsky] "Music presupposes before all else a certain organization in time, a chronomony." The plastic nature of electronic music allows the composer to record all of the values associated with a sound (e.g., pitch, timbre, envelope) in a form that can be shifted and reorganized in time. The ability to modify the time or duration of a sound is one of its most fundamental characteristics. Traditional instrumental music, once recorded, benefits from a similar control over the manipulation of a real-time performance. The equivalency between space and time that Cage attributed to the coming of magnetic tape recording—and which can be extended to any form of analog or digital sound recording or even MIDI [musical instrument digital interface] control signals—has the liberating effect of allowing the composer to place a sound at any point in time at any tempo.

In electronic music, sound itself becomes a theme of composition. The ability to get inside the physics of a sound and directly manipulate its characteristics provides an entirely new resource for composing music. The unifying physics behind all sounds—pitched and unpitched alike—allow a composer to treat all sounds as being materially equal.

Electronic music does not breathe: it is not affected by the limitations of human performance. As Robert Ashley learned about electronic music early on, "It can go on as long as the electricity comes out of the wall." The arc and structure of the music is tolerant of extremes in the duration and flow of sounds. The ability to sustain or repeat sounds for long periods of time—much longer than would be practical for live instrumentalists—is a natural resource of electronic music. In addition to its sustainability, electronic music can play rhythms too complex and rapid for any person to perform. It can play with more than two hands at the same time. The composer is freed of the physical limitations of human performance and can construct new sounds and performances of an intricacy that can only exist as a product of the machine.

Electronic music springs from the imagination. The essence of

electronic music is its disassociation with the natural world. Hearing is a "distance" sense, as opposed to the "proximal" senses of touch and taste. Listening engages the intellect and imagination to interpret what is heard, providing [as Pierre Henry put it,] "only indirect knowledge of what matters—requiring interpretations from knowledge and assumptions, so you can read meaning into the object world." Having little basis in the object world, electronic music becomes the pulse of an intimate and personal reality for the listener. Its source is mysterious. [Henry believed] "It is thought, imagined and engraved in memory. It's a music of memory." In these ways, the human being becomes the living modulator of the machine product, the circuitry dissolves into the spirit of humanness that envelops it.

The Evolution of Sound in the Electronic Age

Mark Prendergast

Irish music critic Mark Prendergast traces the development of what he calls "ambient music" from its be-
ginnings as an esoteric experimental medium for
nineteenth- and twentieth-century avant-garde composers. Prendergast details the key conceptual, technological, and compositional approaches to sound
and music that link romanticism, modernism, and
pop in the Western musical tradition and lead directly to contemporary electronica. This journey
across "the electronic landscape" includes profiles of
three crucial figures in early electronic music: Edgard
Varèse, John Cage, and Karlheinz Stockhausen.

IT WAS THE SUMMER OF 1968. FOR SOME A TIME OF
student unrest, for others a time of discovery. For the German
composer Karlheinz Stockhausen it was a time of intense emotional upheaval. His wife and children had left him. Alone in
his house in Kurten, near Cologne, he contemplated his fate.
Ideas of suicide crossed his mind. He went on hunger strike
and vowed to wait for his family to return. As time passed he
began to write down Japanese-style verses like:

> Play a sound,
> Play it for so long,
> Until you feel that you should stop

or

Mark Prendergast, *The Ambient Century: From Mahler to Trance—The Evolution of
Sound in the Electronic Age*. New York: Bloomsbury, 2000. Copyright © 2000 by Mark
Prendergast. All rights reserved. Reproduced by permission.

Play a vibration in the rhythm of the universe,
Play a vibration in the rhythm of dreaming.

That such words could lead to what Stockhausen termed 'intuitive music' is one of the great fascinations of the twentieth century. Here the composer was getting right inside what it meant to create sound, no longer only concentrating on the external but also the internal processes of becoming aware of what a sound was actually like when first encountered. Or, more accurately, when it was encountered in a different way. Stockhausen played a piano tone after four days of fasting. What he heard changed his life forever.

John Cage had already opened up the world to the reality of silence. During the late 1940s and early 1950s the guru from the American Midwest had pushed music from Eastern-inspired piano pieces of exquisite calm to nothing at all, expressed most concisely in 4' 33". Here, for that duration of time, any performer of any instrument was required to not-play. The music was everything else heard, the Ambient sounds of whatever environment the 'performance' was happening in. Cage had professed that his favourite music was when everything was still, when nothing was attempted. The very sounds of his everyday environment were 'poetry to his ears'.

Responding to the Noise

This non-purposeful acceptance of extraneous sound as music was symptomatic of the increasing hubbub of twentieth-century urban life, where silence as an experience was very rare. To flash back to the mid–nineteenth century, music was something that was experienced as a singular occurrence— once you'd been to the concert hall and heard the orchestra play the symphony, that was it. Music was live or not at all. There was always the piano, but you had to be musically literate to enjoy it. Or at least know somebody who was.

Then along came the player piano, which could record a composer's performance. But then Edison realized you could record music magnetically and away we went towards the capturing of music on record. By the beginning of the twentieth century even [French composer Claude] Debussy was putting his music on to the new medium. Add to that the increasing

popularity of records, the universality of radio, the rise of the tape recorder, the clatter of mass production, the coming of electronic instruments, the increased demand for cars, the universal spread of television and so on—and by John Cage's time modern noise was indeed deafening. Music didn't need to have to jolt people out of their quiet lethargy. It no longer, as it did in the Romantic music of the early nineteenth century, had to carry the sum of all human emotions. Life was hectic enough without more stormy symphonies. Many opted for quiet.

The twentieth century saw two things occur in music which had never happened before. Firstly, music was deconstructed. Before, Western music was quite rigid. The sonata form of the Classical period had specific rules which had to be adhered to. Of course there were exceptional talents but they were constrained within a chosen form. Then the Romantics started to loosen things. [Nineteenth-century German composer Richard] Wagner's grandiose operatic orchestration and [Anton] Bruckner and [Gustav] Mahler pushed the symphony to its limits so that by the end of the nineteenth century it began to creak under its own weight. Then along came [French composer Erik] Satie, Debussy and [Maurice] Ravel with a lighter touch. They wrote more accessible melodies in shorter forms which openly embraced modernity and the need to look beyond parochialism to the riches to be found in other cultures such as the Orient. As a boy in New England Charles Ives would hear his bandleader father's experiments in overlapping the sounds of different marching bands playing different tunes. In France, [Olivier] Messiaen would show that sound could possess rich colours if exotic scales were used. [Arnold] Schoenberg and his pupils of the Second Viennese School tore up the rule book on music and rewrote it imposing upon it a destabilizing force known as Serialism.

As old musical ideas began to be supplanted by new, a second radical change occurred—and this was in the very way music was generated. Composers and musicians began to be fascinated by the nature of individual tones. Serialism, in its dislocative way, had thrown up an interest in the essence of a single sound. The leaders of the post–Second World War avant-garde in Europe, such as Stockhausen, [Pierre] Schaeffer and [Edgard] Varèse, seized on new electronic equipment and

began to experiment with tape recorders. New qualities in sound were perceived, new tonalities divorced from any traditional acoustic instruments were realized. [American inventor Lee] De Forest's invention of the valve in the 1920s had made amplification possible. This, coupled with the concept of the sound environment, made for some spectacular results. The work of Varèse and [Iannis] Xenakis in the pointed Philips pavilion at the 1958 World Fair in Brussels became a twentieth-century archetype of progress married to artistic achievement.

Many, feeling the tug of technological evolution, had campaigned for new musical means. Debussy famously wrote of the century of aeroplanes deserving a music of its own. Varèse saw that electronics could free music from the shackles of the past. The conductor Leopold Stokowski saw a future in which music would be generated by hitherto unknown means. But it took time for technology to catch up with ideas. There were many brave and interesting attempts at creating music machines. In the 1920s both the Theremin and Ondes Martenot were valid sources of novel electronic sound. But it wasn't until the tape experiments of Schaeffer and others that it was realized that a device would have to be built to handle all aspects of organizing and creating music. Hence the arrival of the first synthesizer in the US in the early 1950s. But, as with the computers of the period, music synthesis was tied to the laboratory or similar locations. Then Bob Moog took synthesizers out of the lab and made them more compact and portable. Electronic means had become accessible to any musician who wanted them. Stockhausen's prediction in 1955 that new electronic instruments would yield 'what no instrumentalist has ever been capable of' was at last becoming a reality.

The importance to twentieth-century music of atmospheric sound, its timbre and personality—indeed its 'Ambience'—is a measure of how much innovative musical ideas intertwined with technological change. The series of quiet, luscious Hispanic-inflected albums which [American jazz trumpeter] Miles Davis made in the late 1950s are a case in point. The spirit of Debussy and Iberian composers such as [Joaquin] Rodrigo infuses this beautiful work but so too does the already impressive state of studio and recording technology of the time. Multi-track recording and editing at the production console, enhanced by

special microphone placement, highlighted qualities in the music that in earlier times would have been buried underneath gramophone crackle and tape hiss. It's true to say that improvements in production and consumption of music allowed quieter, more experimental elements to creep in. Could [Hungarian composer György] Ligeti's beautiful *Lux Aeterna* of 1966 have been rendered credibly on old scratchy 78s?

In the nineteenth century symphonies were often loud and raucous affairs that gave the public a visceral jolt through the sheer dynamic of the orchestra. In the twentieth century rock seemed to take over this function. This left composers free to experiment. Wendy (formerly Walter) Carlos transcribed Bach for Moog synthesizer, Iannis Xenakis used mathematics and computers to generate music. [Contemporary Japanese composer] Toru Takemitsu fused Debussy with his Oriental sensibility in a reverse image of what had occurred at the beginning of the century. Moreover synthesizers became digital, with the ability to sample other instruments through the new microprocessing technology of silicon chips. By the end of the twentieth century music was capable of being rendered via small personal computers through a veritable treasure-trove of new electronic samplers, effects units and complex software. New music no longer needed to shout loud to impress. It could do so quietly through the beautiful textures of new super sound technology.

The dominance of the computer in music at the end of the twentieth century was made possible by developments in software and miniaturization. In sound labs at prestigious places like the Massachusetts Institute of Technology (MIT) huge advances were made in areas such as acoustic modelling and spontaneous musical response. In the first of these fields researchers are coming close to a perfect replication of the human voice, in itself an echo from [filmmaker Stanley] Kubrick's prescient film *2001: A Space Odyssey*, where the fictitious HAL 9000 computer could speak. In the latter field computers are being designed to become more musically intelligent, so that they can accompany a human ensemble or instrumentalist.

Important as these things are to the century of sound they would be just aspects of research and development if it weren't for the fidelity of Compact Disc, or CD. The ability of a reflective disc with a diameter of just four and a half inches to

communicate music in all its recorded perfection has rendered technological advances audible in the home. With better hi-fi systems the listener can hear the subtleties of Ambient sound whether it be by Satie, [English composer Frederick] Delius, Cage or [British musician and composer Brian] Eno. Stockhausen has remastered in digital form his entire life's work for presentation on CD. The availability of so much music on the new sound medium has radically changed people's perception of what music is. The combination of constant reissuing of back-catalogue and newer musical hybrids has blurred old prejudices, making it acceptable to like an eclectic mix of styles. At the end of the twentieth century old categories like jazz, pop and classical no longer really applied. Everything was thrown into the sonic soup by virtue of new digital technology. Over a century music had traversed an electronic landscape and now, by virtue of technology, its very texture, its very essence, had become digitally encoded. The search for newer and newer sounds had opened up music to the endless possibilities of Ambient sound. Now, the bleeding heart of electronic progress had, by its very nature, rendered all recorded music, by definition, Ambient. . . .

Edgard Varèse

Beloved of musicians as diverse as Frank Zappa and Stockhausen, Edgard Varèse was one of the twentieth century's great mavericks. In his search for a music of 'beautiful parabolic and hyperbolic curves' Varèse, as early as 1916, was demanding 'new instruments and new technical means' through which to realize 'the organized sounds' of his imagination. He felt that composers and musicians should be able to satisfy every dictate of musical thought and believed that 'electronics could free music'. His life would be a search and a realization of this ideal.

Of Franco-Italian parentage, Varèse was born in Paris in 1883 but moved to Turin with his family while young. He studied harmony and had penned an opera by the age of eleven, but a talent for maths and science led him to study those subjects at Turin University. After returning to Paris in the early 1900s Varèse studied at the Schola Cantorum and the Conservatoire. It was not long before this bright young man attracted the interest of Debussy and Satie and their milieu, which included

the poet Apollinaire and the writer Jean Cocteau. Yet Varèse was more interested in the radical ideas of Ferruccio Busoni after reading the latter's 1907 paper 'Sketch For A New Aesthetic Of Music' and went to Berlin in 1909 to meet the man. There he was stimulated by the Italian's theories of 'free music' and the possibility of musical tones beyond the normal scale (microtonality). . . .

In Varèse's mind sounds that had been heard were old hat. He wrote in an American journal in 1922 that 'speed and synthesis are characteristics of our own epoch'. But since equipment didn't exist to create the new sounds he reasoned he had to invent new sonorities with existing instruments. His flow of compositions through the 1920s and 30s confused many, but Varèse found a willing ally in the conductor Leopold Stokowski. Works like *Amériques* (1921), *Hyperprism* (1923), *Intégrales* (1924) and *Ionisation* (1931) were all takes on the urban landscape, using percussion and strange instrumental combinations to convey, through 'beams of sound', a 'music of the fourth dimension'. Varèse's use of sound blocks and extreme rhythmic changes made his music a challenge and often caused uproar in audiences. Only the short four-minute *Density 21.5* for flute could be said to have Ambient properties.

Of more interest was his direct involvement in electronics. In the late 1920s he approached Bell Telephone for the use of a laboratory to research into possible instruments but no funds were available. In 1927 his friend Bertrand had invented the Dynaphone, a dial-operated monophonic oscillation device like the Theremin, and this was showcased in several European cities. The following year Varèse returned to Paris in order to build a studio to develop the instrument and other ideas. Interestingly, he wrote that the studio contained a complete record collection of 'all races, all cultures', so the world's music might have been available for electronic sampling. But in the 1930s Western electronic engineers, although sympathetic to Varèse's aims, were unable to find the finances. His 1933 application to the Guggenheim Foundation for a grant to research into new scales and frequency ranges with the improved Dynaphone was similarly rebuffed. Frustrated, he experimented by playing records backwards, predating later musical trends by over half a century. . . .

The Invention of Environmental Ambience

Varèse's finest achievement was his *Poème electronique* for the Philips pavilion at the Brussels World Fair of 1958. The futuristic pavilion was co-designed by Le Corbusier and the architect-composer Iannis Xenakis and has become a strident historical symbol of post-war modernism. Invited to Eindhoven by Philips, Varèse was provided with a special sound laboratory with the latest equipment and the finest engineers available. There he realized a piece for eleven-channel tape which was relayed through 425 speakers. Sound projection was organized so that the chorus of bells, piano, organs, pulse-generated drums, continuous rhythm and an electronically treated girl's voice could be heard from any angle. Through the use of tape looping, the eight-minute piece could be heard continuously but it was strangely different each time the sequence repeated. This effect was enhanced by an array of coloured lights which projected images in synchronization with the music. In a flash of creative genius, Varèse had invented environmental Ambience. It's estimated that two million people had experienced *Poème electronique* by the end of 1958.

That year Stockhausen met Varèse in New York and declared him 'the father figure of electronic music'. By demanding 'twentieth-century instruments for twentieth-century music', Varèse was practically applying Debussy's dream of a new music. In his writings Varèse precisely predicted the rise of synthesizers and the role of sampling equipment in creating new sounds. His tragedy was that he was too far ahead of his time, without the tools or the finance to realize his dreams. His legacy is more to other musicians than to listeners. What is striking is that his ideas for light and colour projection, his use of records and the sound environment of *Poème electronique* were a blueprint for Ambient Techno Music of the 1990s. On the death of this pioneer in 1965, Stockhausen affirmed both his artistic and human greatness. . . .

John Cage

Through a constellation of musics John Cage became the guru of twentieth-century Ambient composition. Deriving inspiration from Erik Satie, Charles Ives and then Arnold Schoenberg, Cage did more than anybody else before him to isolate

the quality of sound. In his quest for the ultimate sound he arrived at silence. In his mind there was no difference between
noise, sound and silence—all were poetry to his ears. His presence throughout the twentieth century initiated much experiment in the fields of electronic music, mixed-media, total Serialism (where an attempt is made to measure everything in
music) and environmental music. He was a beacon to talents
as diverse as Pierre Boulez, Stockhausen, La Monte Young,
David Tudor, The Velvet Underground, Brian Eno and many
more. Above all he opened huge causeways for the dissemina-
tion of Ambient music. In 1989 he said: 'People will often opt
for quiet sounds. The awful presence of intention in music
makes the non-intentional Ambient sound more useful. It is
more possible to live affirmatively if you find environmental
sound beautiful.' . . .

From 1934 until 1937 Cage took music lessons with
Schoenberg in California. Initially the Viennese inventor of
Serialism said that his would-be pupil couldn't afford his fees.
The ever-charming Cage admitted that he had no money but
pledged to devote his life to music, and Schoenberg took him
on. Already writing in the serial style, Cage had great difficulty
mastering harmony or chordal progression. Schoenberg felt
that his student was beating his head against a brick wall. One
day the composer sent Cage to the blackboard in order to answer a musical problem. When Cage found one, Schoenberg
demanded another. When Cage answered this, Schoenberg
demanded another, and then another. Frustrated, Cage added,
'Why?' To which Schoenberg requested an underlying principle. This questioning of what music actually was would stay
with Cage for the rest of his life. He worshipped Schoenberg's
ingenuity and the latter said famously of Cage that he was
much 'more than a musician but an inventor—of genius'.

As a composer and accompanist at dance classes at the
Cornish School in Seattle, Cage realized that his experience
with Schoenberg had made him see that listeners could ac-
tively choose what to listen to at the point of listening. In 1937
he wrote a brilliant lecture titled 'The Future Of Music
(Credo)', which he delivered at the school. This predicted the
rise of electronic music: 'Through the aid of electrical instruments we will reach a music which will make available all

sounds that can be heard.' Cage talked of any sounds or noises being capable of electrical reproduction 'within or beyond the reach of the imagination'. In his mind electronics opened up 'the entire field of sound, the entire field of time where no rhythm would be beyond the composer's earth'. Significantly he saw conventional use of inventions like the Theremin as being redundant, and looked instead to possibilities in radio, disc and film technology. These were explored in a series of radical pieces called *Imaginary Landscapes* (1939–52). *No. 1* (1939) featured vari-speed turntables playing RCA test recordings. *No. 2* (1942) featured sounds produced by amplifying wire coil. *No. 3*, from the same year, included audio-frequency oscillaton, amplified contact mikes and vari-speed turntables, while *No. 4* (1951) featured twelve radio sets being continuously retuned. For the last of the series, *Imaginary Landscape No. 5* (1952), Cage, with the help of Earle Brown and Bebe Barron, collaged forty-two jazz records into a huge tape mix. . . .

It was in 1942, on his arrival in New York, that the final piece of the jigsaw would slot into place. At the home of [Surrealist painter] Max Ernst, Cage and his wife Xenia met two other founders of the Surrealist movement in painting, André Breton and Marcel Duchamp. As early as 1913 Duchamp had written a piece of music using 'chance' as a compositional tool. Cage and he immediately clicked and would in the future play many chess games together. Later during the same gathering Cage would meet the Irish-American choreographer Merce Cunningham. Their relationship would blossom, Cage becoming musical director of the Merce Cunningham Dance Company until 1968 and living openly with Cunningham from 1947 after divorcing his wife in 1945.

If the dance context was fertile for Cage's fervent experimentalism, New York gave him more opportunities. He studied Zen Buddhism in 1946–7, and its calming aspect is apparent in the contemplative *Nocturne* (for violin and piano). In 1948 Cage hit his zenith as a composer. During a year when he organized an Erik Satie festival at Black Mountain College came two seven-minute piano pieces, *Dream* and *In A Landscape*, whose lack of adornment echoes Satie but whose drift reflects Cage's growing Zen orientation. As his scores became more colourful and graphic, he spent nine months tossing coins, as outlined by

the Chinese oracle the *I Ching*, to create charts for his forty-six-minute piano piece *Music Of Changes*, written in 1951 for David Tudor, a Philadelphian new musician who was involved in presenting all of Cage's works up to 1970. . . .

During the 1960s Cage became a hero of the times. As Professor of Advanced Studies at the University of Connecticut he had academic clout while his soft-spoken, humorous persona and mental brilliance made him shine wherever he went. Stockhausen, who always admired him, felt Cage was 'spiritually very consequent'. Such pieces as *Cartridge Music* (for turntable cartridges and other media) and 'HPSCHD' (for harpsichords, tapes, images and computer generated permutations courtesy of Lejaren Hiller), written in 1960 and 1968 respectively, were electronic landmarks demonstrating an acute mind looking forward into the multi-media future. . . .

Karlheinz Stockhausen

One of the most significant figures in twentieth-century music, Karlheinz Stockhausen was the first composer to realize the dream of 'pure' electronic music. His inventions of the 1950s catapulted him to world fame where he became the spokesman of the post-war avant-garde. As the 1960s dawned Stockhausen's brand of open and improvised music became associated with hippiedom—he was often criticized for his association with the likes of The Grateful Dead and his Zen Buddhist-influenced musings. Yet here was one of the most acute and rigorous minds in modern composition acknowledging the musicality of the new psychedelia. His *Gesang der Jünglinge* (*Song Of The Youths*) and *Hymnen* (*Anthems*) both affected The Beatles. Stockhausen was a friend of John Lennon, and the German's influence can be heard on the group's extraordinary single 'Strawberry Fields Forever', the 'Revolution 9' collage (on *The White Album*) and on the 1967 album *Sgt. Pepper's Lonely Hearts Club Band*, the cover of which features a photographic tribute to Stockhausen. One of the foremost exponents of live electronic music, Stockhausen pursued an endless quest for new sounds, leading to the growth of World Music. In the 1990s his opinion was still being sought by Techno and Ambient musicians as to the validity of their work. . . .

Nineteen fifty-one was the turning point for the young

German. Taken up by Herbert Eimert, a critic at West German Radio (WDR) in Cologne who admired Schoenberg, Stockhausen was invited to Darmstadt, where a series of new music summer courses inspired by Messiaen had started. Pierre Schaeffer, the Italian avantist Luigi Nono and the physicist Werner Meyer-Eppler (whose interest was in chance or aleatory music) were some of the people Stockhausen met that summer. Eimert and Meyer-Eppler would initiate the founding of an electronic studio at WDR that same year. Around that time Stockhausen graduated with distinction.

In 1953 he attended Messiaen's analysis classes at the Paris Conservatoire. The Frenchman's teaching, based on innovation by example and understanding, was an inspiration for Stockhausen. Messiaen, for his part, was convinced that the twenty-five-year-old German was 'an absolute genius'. *Kreuzspiel* (*Crossplay*) of 1951, which isolated points of sound, had certainly been Stockhausen's eleven-minute kick in the face to Romanticism. While in Paris Stockhausen met Pierre Boulez and visited Pierre Schaeffer's studio at Radio France. Soon he was working there on sound analysis and spent just one month coming up with *Study*, a piece which combined electronic sound with concrete music and mixed frequency generator noise with prepared piano. Schaeffer, in search of a wider palette of sound, wasn't impressed and Stockhausen soon found himself back in Germany. . . .

An Electronic Mass

Between 1954 and 1956 Stockhausen pursued further studies at Bonn University. He was drawn by Meyer-Eppler's acoustical research into vocoders and sonic measurement. Also stimulated by John Cage's interest in 'chance' music, Stockhausen would soon meet the American and Edgard Varèse, both of whom he greatly admired. Fascinated by the versatility of tape, in 1955 Stockhausen wanted to create an electronic mass for Cologne Cathedral. The idea was rejected but the composer set about writing a section: *The Song Of The Youths In The Fiery Furnace*, later abbreviated to the famous *Song Of The Youths* (*Gesang der Jünglinge*). Using pulse generator, volume meter and feedback filter, Stockhausen spent six months breaking down every element of human speech and matching it to every

conceivable sound from sine tone to white noise. The result of this painstaking process was only five minutes of valuable sound; but by May 1956 he had completed a piece lasting thirteen minutes and fourteen seconds. The debut performance of *Song Of The Youths*, projected through five loudspeakers at the broadcasting studio of WDR in Cologne, caused uproar and applause. Electronic music was here to stay and Stockhausen's name would reverberate around the world.

Stockhausen attracted many new musicians and composers to Cologne, including the Hungarian György Ligeti. His next important piece was *Kontakte* (*Contacts*), where tape loops were used to create a kaleidoscope of electronic sounds. Here the acceleration of tape caused pulses to become rhythms, rhythms to become pitches, pitches to become timbres. He famously used a rotary table to splash sound around four different microphones. Photographs of the composer at the time show him lost in the hub of WDR's electronic equipment. And after six months of intense work the premiere of this thirty-five-minute piece in Cologne in 1960 proved that Stockhausen was the leader of a new musical revolution.

In Cologne he attracted the interest of many, including the German social philosopher and musicologist Theodor Adorno, the musician David Tudor and a young painter named Mary Bauermeister, who would eventually become his second wife. Meanwhile others raged against Stockhausen's music, the German press describing it as 'a denaturalized montage of noises derived from physics'. . . .

Near the end of 1995 the composer was contacted by the BBC and asked his opinion of new Techno music by such Ambient trend-setters of the time as Richie Hawtin, Aphex Twin and Scanner. He was happy to see the young still experimenting and looking for new sounds, as in the telephone sampled work of Scanner. For nearly half a century the guru of Cologne, in long-sleeved Mexican shirts and with flowing blond hair, has exerted a powerful effect on the development of electronic and Ambient music. For Stockhausen the way ahead is clear and unbounded: 'I just don't see any limits in the foreseeable future.'

From Recording to Remix: The Technologies of Electronic Music

Hillegonda C. Rietveld

Without technological developments in sound recording, synthesizing, and computer processing, electronic music would not be possible. Hillegonda C. Rietveld, senior lecturer in media studies at South Bank University in London, England, introduces readers to the specific technologies that have given form to electronic music and provided the basis for the emergence of both the club DJ and the do-it-yourself laptop music collagist. Rietveld examines a varied selection of key figures in the popularization of electronic music—from the Beach Boys and Kraftwerk to Depeche Mode and DJ Spooky—and demonstrates how particular technological innovations shaped and expanded electronic music's palette as well as its appeal to DJs and dancers alike.

THE DEVELOPMENT OF ELECTRONIC MUSICAL instruments has been of major importance while from the late 80s onwards, computer technology has made a major impact. Samplers and computerised sequencers are standard equipment in any studio which produces dance music. Both have different functions in the process of digital recording. A sampler is a digital recording device with which one can manipu-

■

Hillegonda C. Rietveld, *This Is Our House: House Music, Cultural Spaces, and Technologies.* Aldershot, UK: Ashgate, 1998. Copyright © 1998 by Hillegonda C. Rietveld. All rights reserved. Reproduced by permission.

late the sound textures that have been recorded with it. The sequencer is able to record, memorise and replay a sequence of notes in the way that a word processor works with a written text. When programmed it can trigger sound generating modules such as synthesizers, drum machines and samplers, in a similar manner as a word processing application which triggers a printer. The sequenced sound pattern is communicated via a cable network currently called MIDI, or Musical Instrument Digital Interface. . . .

Soundwaves and Synthesizers

The synthesizer started its life in 1929 when an instrument appeared that had four oscillators, which were controlled by paper rolls. In the same year the Hammond organ was first produced, which in terms of the way that it works may also be seen as a precursor of the synthesizer. Through the ecclesiastical connotations of the organ the Hammond was first seen in churches and due to its relatively low cost gained popularity in the gospel churches of the USA and Jamaica, whereby it influenced the musical styles of African cultural descent, such as soul and R&B. Another electronic sound generator at the beginning of the history of the synthesizer is the Theremin. This device electronically produces a single sinus wave which can be controlled by the distance between an extending pole and the hand of the musician. The resulting sound is comparable with that of an electronic fretless stringed instrument with a single string, whereby the 'width' or 'vowel' sound can be varied by changing the shape of the hand. It took until 1954 before a computerized synthesising instrument was developed, which was the RCA Mark II Columbia-Princeton synthesizer. However, this instrument, which could be controlled with a type of keyboard like the Hammond organ, filled up several rooms. Finally, in 1964, [notes Bernard Krause] the first practical synthesizer was put on the market by Moog:

> Donald Buchla and Robert Moog produced the modular synthesizer with integrated circuitry (so) that electronic music leapt beyond the bounds of academia into the mainstream of modern music.

The sound-waves, which oscillators of the Moog produced,

could be manipulated by filters. Other companies followed on a small scale, but the technology was often only used as an effect like The Beach Boys did with the Theremin on *Good Vibrations*.

In the early 70s electronic music technologies became part of the popular idiom. On the mainland of Europe a combination of the availability of capital combined with an avant garde sensibility facilitated the existence of projects like Tangerine Dream and White Noise which appeared on radio programmes like the Dutch *Super-clean Dream-machine* in the mid-70s. Kraftwerk were one of the more prominent danceable electronic music outfits, whose recordings *Autobahn* and *Trans Europe Express* heralded the beginning of electronic trance dance music, which is, [according to David Toop]

> as Kraftwerk's Ralf Hutter described it to (David Toop) in 1987: Letting yourself go. Sit on the rails and ch-ch-ch-ch-ch. Just keep going. Fade in and fade out rather than trying to be dramatic or trying to implant into the music a logical order which I think is ridiculous. In our society everything is in motion. Music is a flowing artform.

The Italian Giorgio Moroder produced electronic studio based dance music with a similar cyclical groove, but added a 'sexy' 'black' female voice to his music, like the 17 minute *Love To Love You Baby* (1975), featuring disco Diva Donna Summer in a project, which may be described as the throbbing predecessor of electronic pop dance outfits. The Euro-disco format often consists of one or two male electronic composers, preferably fronted by a 'black' female singer. David Toop comments on European disco music in the 70s:

> Although the African component, the cyclic trance rhythm, was central to disco, the African-American gospel element was optional. Europeans, often African or Afro-Caribbean Europeans, found themselves welcome at the party. Their talent for the endless loop and the chant, along with an un-American angle on sexuality, overrode previous difficulties with language and expression. This was the new, ecstatic language of continuous motion.

. . . As electronic music technology gradually became more sophisticated as well as cheaper, the pop sensibility of this

technology increased with English outfits such as The Human League and Depeche Mode in the late 70s and the early 1980s. Although synthesizers originally produced distinct electronic sounds which suited the futuristic fantasies of the avant garde, [Andrew Goodwin explains that] they became popular when they were able to 'simulate the sounds of conventional instruments'. In 1964 it became possible to reproduce conventional sounds with the Mellotron, an instrument with a keyboard which triggers magnetic tape loops with pre-recorded sounds like choirs and string quartets as well as special effects such as a thunder storm. In the 70s it was used by progressive rock groups. In a sense this was a precursor of the keyboard with 'realistic' sounds. Since the late 80s it has been possible to buy keyboards with pre-recorded sampled sounds which have been manipulated and synthesised.

To avoid repetitiveness in sound textures, however, one could buy new sound chips and cards or otherwise synthesise new sounds, depending on what type of synthesising module is used. Most of the older synthesizers had no pre-programmed or sampled sounds but for a lot of people this made the synthesizer 'inaccessible'. In 1994 there were roughly two types of synthesizers; the programmable synthesising module and the populist pre-programmed sound module which often contains sampled sounds. Korg for example brought out a 'sister' digital keyboard to the M1 called the Wavestation which allows for the synthesising of a huge variety of sounds, including the 'classic analogue' sounds of synthesizers from the 80s.

Another possibility is to sample one's own sound textures. Although its price put it out of reach for most people when it appeared on the market in 1979, the Fairlight Computer Musical Instrument was the first commercially available sampling device, followed by the cheaper Emulator, Synclavier, Ensoniq Mirage and Akai. The sampler allows one to enlarge the sound palette to a seemingly infinite range of possibilities. Single drum sounds, small segments of instrumental sounds such as a guitar or a stringed instrument or perhaps the sound of a pen hitting a bottle can be manipulated and used as source material for new textures.

To producers and remixers the sampler is also a useful tool which enables the reconstruction of a song. Parts of a song

which are repeated in its structure, such as the chorus, only have to be recorded once. Often the most successful parts of the recording are sampled and inserted where they are needed as well. Remixers use a similar method to create a new track, using only a few key elements of the original recordings. Sometimes only a few words from the original vocals are used as a rhythmical device for what is otherwise an instrumental dub. This technique follows from the working method of the DJ, who sometimes uses the sampler as an extension of DJ equipment. . . .

Existing songs and tracks can be cut up and parts such as hook lines can be recorded on the sampler, after which the samples could be triggered in a new order by the sequencer. In this manner, a new version can be obtained with the addition of a 'fresh' drum-machine track and a certain number of synthesizers. When this type of 'remix' has not been commissioned by the original songwriting perfomer or by other representatives which own part of the copyright of a song or its recording, its commercial release may be stigmatised as an act of theft and the product will be regarded as a bootleg.

Two Turntables and a Micro-Revolution

Without a DJ tradition of using recorded music as elements of a soundscape for a dance, equipment such as samplers would not have gained the importance as they have now within dance club music. In 1877, Thomas Alva Edison invented the phonograph or 'voice-writer', which [according to Michael Chanan] was 'the forerunner of today's record player', while Edison's colleague Emil Berliner created the first 'disk-type record' [according to Radcuffe Joe]. Gramophone records have been commercially available in the USA since 1894. During the first half of the twentieth century, especially after 1936, the use of jukeboxes in public spaces in the USA enabled (dance) music which was from another area or which was lavishly orchestrated to be accessible to a wider audience; live performances are relatively expensive and logistically cumbersome in comparison. Although even before 1940 in France records were played in clubs by a DJ, in the USA it took until the late 1950s before the DJ took over from the jukebox. A major progression has been the specific use of two record players in the 60s to en-

able the DJ to cue up the next record. With the addition of felt mats on top of the turntables one could cue the record without having to jam the mechanical parts of the record player. Using two record players in combination with a DJ mixer and a pair of head phones, the DJ is able to blend one record into another at the correct speed, making the beats of the rhythms join up, or inserting parts of one record on top of another one. It has therefore become possible for the mixing of records to become a sophisticated skill, to the extent that DJ Spooky claims: 'Gimme two records and I'll make you a universe.'

In the 70s specialist turntables called decks came on the market. Since the late 70s the Japanese have produced Technics SL1200 and SL1210, which have become the most popular amongst professionals. Decks are different from domestic turntables in that they allow the DJ to be in control of the change in speeds between records. Technics has a patent on its magnetic drive device, which is useful for several reasons; the turntable can accelerate from being stationary to its desired speed within a small fraction of time and while the motor still runs, one is able to stop the record by hand or to move forward or backward without causing friction to its mechanical parts. DJs were enabled to begin competing with each other with sometimes acrobatic skills, especially in the hip hop scene. . . .

In the case of house music and related musical forms the slow mix is usually favoured over the cut and mix styles of hip hop and some dance hall reggae. Since songs and tracks are made to overlap, a sense of harmony may be achieved if the melody scales of the different songs fit. Although there are arguments on the subject amongst DJs, this is not of primary importance to a groove based dance music like house. In house music one may find DJ mixes and even records produced by professional DJs which have a vocal which seems 'out of tune' with the bass line. A tendency to foreground rhythms and textures, rather than melodies, has been strengthened by this groove-centred DJ method throughout the 1980s.

Magnetic Tape and the 'Dub' Track

Manipulation of recorded sounds in the studio became a possibility after the Second World War when magnetic tape, invented in 1928 by Fritz Pleumer in Germany, was used for mu-

sic recording. In 1947 the magnetic tape recorder was used for the first time in a commercial context for the American Bing Crosby radio show, although [as David Harker notes] it was 'then transferred to 16-inch disc for transmission'. In the same year Capitol started to use tape for their recordings and in 1950 tape recording replaced disc recording altogether both in the USA and the UK. Experimental composers were keen to play around with the new technology, so for example in the early 1950s [Pierre] Schaffer and [Pierre] Henri created musique concrete by manipulating recorded sounds in the ORTF Studios in Paris, where sounds, such as voices, were cut, filtered and run at different speeds. On the other side of the Atlantic, during the 1970s and 1980s in the USA, teenagers with DJ aspirations, but who could not afford records or record decks, would construct 'scratch' pause-button sound collages with the help of (preferably) two audio cassette decks, mainly using material recorded from radio shows, such as dance club music and hip hop. Closer to the locality from where I am writing, in London recording tape was used during the 1960s, to provide non-stop music at parties and clubs which was not possible when the DJ used only one deck. From there the idea sparked for Londoners that two record decks could be useful to provide the same effect, except that the choice of records could be adapted to the mood of the audience.

In 1958, the first Shure Brothers 4-track tape recorders became available in the USA, which enabled different instruments to be recorded on separate tracks in a parallel fashion (as opposed to the serial collage methods described above). It was also possible to overdub parts of the recording. This led to the possibility of creating (instrumental) 'dub' tracks. By the late 1960s in Jamaica, due to a lack of finance for studio time or new tapes, different singers used the same instrumental track as backing for the recording of their own song; the individual vocal performances could vary dramatically. This type of recording performance was based on the practice of Jamaican sound system parties, where instrumental tracks were played by the DJ with either an MC or singer providing vocal entertainment to dedicated crowds of dancers. With the use of multi-track recording techniques, these instrumental tracks developed into the sophisticated overlaying of sounds of dub

which were created in the early 1970s with King Tubby in the vanguard. In New York the development of instrumental dance club tracks trailed behind the Jamaican dubs. Although Walter Gibbons produced the first soundscape in disco with Double Exposure's *Ten Percent* (1976), adding extra parts wherein the track was stripped to its percussive groove, it was not until the early 80s that the instrumental made its appearance as a dub mix in New York club music. DJ, producer and one time A&R [artist and repertoire agent] for disco label Prelude Francois Kervorkian remembered:

> Around 1980/82 we were aware of Mad Professor, King Tubby and Black Uhuru's *In Dub* album. It was the first time in New York we'd made that reggae connection and so we used it in an uptempo style.

A host of separate developments in instrumental dance music creation such as German proto trance, Italian Euro-disco, English HiNRG, English electronic pop, Jamaican dub, Chicago DJ tracks and New York dance club instrumentals were beginning to cross over on the dance floors of New York, Chicago and Europe in the early 1980s. This network of connections became the beginning of dance music like, for example, house music as we know it today. This would not have been possible without the technologies as described above.

Do-It-Yourself Technologies

Digital recording has enabled the increase of the possibility of cultural and generic cross-over as well as an increased speed in the time of reaction on different musical products. Initially this type of technology was developed by the end of the 70s in order to overcome the static noises and the distortions which troubled analogue recording methods. As has been the case with all other (re)productive musical technologies, although exclusive at first, sequencers, samplers and DAT machines can now be afforded by the person 'on the street' at a grassroots level. A composition could be created at home without being dependent on large investments by the major music industry and therefore without their interference. . . .

The home production of CDs straight from one's PC (personal computer) has become a possibility. A consequence of the

possibility of independent home recording is that the production of recorded music has been democratised; a less censored form of music can appear on the market. The early house tracks from Chicago, with their sexually explicit lyrics and raw unpolished productions are an example of this, as are references to male 'gay' relationships in New York club music, the hard hitting Dutch gabber [aka gabba] house or the manic British rave tracks which contain sly references to the (illegal) use of the dance drug ecstasy. Since it is now possible to release one's own record and distribute it either oneself or through an independent distributor, a kind of grassroots folk sensibility has been returned to popular music. Tracks are produced for a home market and have acquired local characteristics, such as the use of Dutch language on some Dutch techno tracks. On the other hand, in a global market characterised by rapid exchanges in communication, the use of similar technologies and spaces of consumption has made it possible for certain tracks to 'make a cross over' from one scene to another. Despite local differences, dance music which can be grouped together under the tag 'house' is part of an international cultural aesthetic which shares certain formal qualities. Its differences are like accents and colloquialisms which bring welcome fresh ideas and which allow dance music to mutate into new directions.

EXAMINING POP CULTURE

The Rave Scene

The Rise of DJ Culture

Dave Haslam

Dave Haslam was a DJ at the Haçienda, a club in
Manchester, England, during the late 1980s. The
Haçienda was the epicenter of the rave scene in England at that time. In the following selection, Haslam
focuses on Sasha, a contemporary superstar DJ, and
reflects on the emergence of DJs during the rave era.
As the dance music craze grew, DJs rose from relative
anonymity to the status of international pop superstars. Some became millionaires through their various
business ventures, which included recording and producing records, establishing their own record labels,
and landing lucrative endorsement deals. However,
the true value of a DJ, Haslam notes, lies in his or
her ability to work a crowd by reading its mood and
coaxing it into action.

SOME WEEKS SASHA CAN TRAVEL UPWARDS OF
eighteen thousand miles, DJ-ing in Mexico City, then New
York, returning to his home in Henley on Thames, on to Fab-
ric in London, and then a headline slot at one of Europe's
dance music festivals.

Sasha was one of the first British DJs to command fat fees
for turning up to clubs with a box or two of records, and then
playing them. Putting one record on after the other seems
such a simple business, but now dance music and club culture
have grown so big, DJs are working at the centre of something
lucrative, global and powerful.

Sasha has been at the top of the DJ league for twelve, thir-

∎

Dave Haslam, *Adventures on the Wheels of Steel*. London, UK: Fourth Estate, 2002.
Copyright © 2002 by Dave Haslam. Reproduced by permission.

teen years. Before him there were dozens of DJs with no commercial profile but lots of credibility, or famous, but embarrassing, Radio One [a BBC youth-oriented program] DJs. There had been DJs playing in underground gay clubs or semi-legal parties in New York, and British DJs with a cult following on the various specialist soul and hip hop scenes, but Sasha was the first to have both commercial profile and credibility.

His rise to fame wasn't manufactured. It started with stories of queues outside obscure venues, and clubbers who had travelled across Northern England to hear him play. This was in Stoke and elsewhere around 1990, 1991. Only a few years before nearly all club disc jockeys talked between records, told bad jokes, and ran wet t-shirt competitions. In the modern era the big name DJs like Sasha make a living just playing records; their reputation, or otherwise, is down to their taste, their skill—mixing, blending and chopping the records, building and controlling the momentum of the crowd—and success, or luck, in managing their career.

I'm on Sasha's trail, meeting up with him a few hours before he's due to play a set to two thousand people in Glasgow. His room in the Devonshire Gardens hotel is the size of a small club. It also has a fully stocked mini-bar and a four poster bed. Sasha has just checked in—with his mate Sparrow and three girls from America called Zoe, Charity and Jennifer—and he's showered and got changed. Now he's sorting out his records. Meticulously he goes through the two boxes he has with him, putting the right records into the right sleeves, dumping to one side a dozen or so records that he definitely won't need later. He is imagining his set at the Arches tonight. He works his way through the boxes, having a quiet drink, while Sparrow bounces around regaling me with his stories about the time he and Sasha shared a flat in Salford.

At half past midnight a driver knocks on the door, and Sasha tells him he'll be ready in five minutes. Twenty minutes later we're heading out of the room, down the stairs and into a Shogun parked just up the road. Charity is handing out very minty mints. I'm carrying one of Sasha's records. Tonight I am Sasha's box boy.

From the front door, the club doesn't look like much, but as we're ushered along the corridors leading from the entrance

to the far side, our walk takes us through crowds of excited people. Many of them call out and cheer as they spy Sasha surrounded by us, his scurrying entourage; "Sasha, hey Sash-aah!" they shout. The main auditorium is packed.

A Cultural Shift

This is a new kind of pop stardom. For young dance music fans, DJ-ing is a route to 'Top of the Pops' as well as a lucrative career presiding over club dancefloors, gathering air miles and emptying mini-bars. The profile of DJs has been boosted since Sasha's early days by the success of recording artists with their roots in DJ-ing (like the Chemical Brothers, Fatboy Slim, and Basement Jaxx).

It's a shift in music culture; more pairs of decks [turntables] are now sold each year than electric guitars. As part of the [British] Labour Government's New Deal in 1999 specially researched information packs were produced giving career guidance for aspiring DJs.

The vocabulary of DJ-ing has also seeped out into the wider world. In a KFC commercial the breakdancing Colonel announces a 'hot new remix' of his Twister, whatever that is. DJs the Dreem Team have inspired footballers like Kieron Dyer and Emile Heskey to celebrate their goals with a DJ mime, one hand over their left ear like a headphone and the other spinning a record on the deck. Rave classics turn up in the most unlikely places; Jaydee's 'Plastic Dreams' was a cult club record nearly ten years ago, now it's a favoured backdrop to British television's Italian football coverage.

The Birth of the Rave Era

In Britain the key moment of change, the birth of the rave era, is generally reckoned to be the Summer of 1988. We'd had hip hop and electro, now stripped down, computer-aided, often instrumental, house and techno from America was energising a new generation who rejected rock bands and live gigs, and took to the dancefloor instead. It was all a long way from the structure and sounds of a conventional rock song—or, for that matter, the classic soul song—no verse, chorus, verse, chorus. At the same time, ecstasy use was changing clubs forever.

I was DJ-ing at the Hacienda, in Manchester, at the end of

the 1980's. The Hacienda had been open since 1982, but it was only after 1986 that the policy of the club shifted from being primarily a gig venue to doing club nights. By 1987 we were having some great, packed nights there, but once ecstasy arrived—in the early months of 1988—it was if everything moved up a level; a night at the Hacienda went from being a great night out, to an emotional, life-changing experience.

There was no plan, no one around had any idea where it would lead; all we knew was that dancefloor was where it was at, and these new records were making every old record, especially every old rock record sound dull and old fashioned.

The spooky noises and the break downs seemed made for the Hacienda, a cavernous old warehouse. House music embraced a new generation of computer technology, more and more boxes of computer trickery emitting the requisite throbbing beats and subsonic squelching basslines; literally new noises, a new pallet. We had entered the digital era, and our lives were being played out to a new soundtrack.

When instrumental dance music emerged, it was greeted like abstract art in the Sixties, with a similar grappling for points of reference, human interest, narrative. Now Mark Rothko is on your living room wall and 'Plastic Dreams' on your TV.

In the space of just over a decade club culture has gone from being popular but marginalised to being thoroughly mainstream. Dance music magazines are paper shop best sellers; nightclubs have been key catalysts in the regeneration of British cities (the Hacienda in Manchester and 'Cream' in Liverpool being two examples).

Resistance to Rave

Voices raised in opposition to dance music have been heard since people first started gathering in rooms to dance. Dancing was always connected with morals; the puritan strain in society has always found dancing, like fun, to be a suspect activity, and back in 1988 the rave scene met with some resistance. Decades before acid house, a queue of people waiting to go into a room to dance—especially to dance to a DJ—had been an affront to the sensibilities of countless rock musicians, right wing newspapers, left wing social critics, policemen, politi-

cians, and church leaders. In fact, their opponents were the first people to recognise the power of DJs as taste makers and role models. In 1958 a judge in Cambridge, Massachusetts commented that the "leadership of the disk jockey had dangerously supplanted the leadership of the good elements in the community among these impressionable teenagers".

Anti-disco prejudice occasionally came from less expected sources. Reverend Jesse Jackson entered the fray in 1976. He pointed to evidence from a survey of a thousand girls at a North Hollywood high school which had found that ninety per cent of them had had sexual intercourse whilst listening to "songs with suggestive lyrics and rhythms". He was particularly fearful about the possible effects of KC & the Sunshine Band's hit song '(Shake Shake Shake) Shake Your Booty'.

In 1988 Peter Powell, a DJ on Radio One, described house music as "mass zombiedom" and campaigned to have it taken off the airwaves. But the forces of D.I.S.C.O have triumphed. Now Radio One embraces house music and the club scene, employing DJs with dancefloor pedigrees, promoting nights in Ibiza, and broadcasting live from clubs.

International Superstars

The likes of Sasha, Paul Van Dyk, Paul Oakenfold, Pete Tong, and Danny Tenaglia are big name DJs with their own devoted following, and the music magazines are filled with heated debates on their various qualities. Today dozens of international DJs crisscross the world; check your club listings guide and you'll find DJs from Holland playing in Ireland or Yorkshire; DJs from New York in Manchester or Sheffield; DJs from Manchester in Israel or New Zealand; DJs from Glasgow in London; London DJs in Finland, Ibiza, or San Francisco.

At a big gig you get treated like royalty, like a popstar. At 'Cream' someone will pick you up from the hotel, someone will carry your records from the car to the DJ booth, the doormen will be on hand to escort you. The first time I played at 'Cream' I was desperate for a drink, so I leaned over to the lighting guy and did what I normally do in the situation, gave him a tenner and asked him to get us both a drink. "Is your fridge empty?", he asked, pointing to a white cupboard behind me, under the ledge I'd put my record boxes on. Inside, the

club had provided me with a crate of Budweiser, chilling. You get the star treatment. You might have to stay up all night. You might arrive at a club and the promoter's runner gets sent to see if you want any Class A drugs. You might lose a night's sleep. You may end up at a party in some place you don't know in a town you've never visited before. You might spend one early morning walking through Detroit with two girls whose names will always escape you. You might get back to a hotel at five in the morning and feel an inexplicable urge to rearrange the potted plants in the hotel foyer. There might be a bunch of you in the same hotel; it might be you and the Dope Smugglaz and Parks & Wilson. You could be the one who gets called by reception early in the morning; "I think your colleague Mr Wilson has lost a shoe."

Like the popstars they seem to be replacing, DJs get tempted into late-night shenanigans; a life of decks and drugs and posh hotels. Some inhabit the same celebrity bubble as film stars, supermodels and TV personalities. Like popstars, DJs get some fame and surround themselves with yes men. Ego takes over. Some of them forget that a great club night is a two-way collaboration, with the DJ focusing and manipulating the energy of the crowd, teasing noise, reactions and emotions out of them. A DJ without a crowd is just someone with some records.

But most working DJs aren't in the big league. Whilst Paul Oakenfold can be paid anything from £5,000 upwards for an appearance, an established DJ on the circuit will be getting somewhere between £400 and £800, and your local Ritz jock will be earning around £150. In a good week Sasha can earn something in the region of £15,000. DJs like Paul Oakenfold also, of course, earn extra dollars through remix work and production, the proceeds from record labels, and sponsorship and endorsements.

Humble Beginnings

The power, the fame, the corporate interests; it's all a long way from clubland before acid house. In 1982 Paul Oakenfold was selling sweaters at Woodhouse, then got a job in the A&R department at Champion, then moved on to work for Profile, the New York hip hop label. In 1986 he was trying to help push

Profile in Britain. In 1986 Pete Tong had been a DJ on the soul boy circuit in the South East of England and a staff writer for *Blues & Soul*, but had started working at London Records and had just licensed 'Love Can't Turn Around'. For others, their rise through the ranks had barely started. In 1986 Fatboy Slim—then known as Norman Cook—had three top twenty hits in the jangly guitar group the Housemartins. Sasha in 1986 was working in a fish factory. Since 1988 they have all become

The Importance of 12-inch Vinyl

Kai Fikentscher is an ethnomusicologist whose first book, "You Better Work!": Underground Dance Music in New York City, *examines the history and culture of the dance scene in New York. In this excerpt, Fikentscher describes the central role of the vinyl disk in the development of dance music.*

The development of the 12-inch single and its almost immediate appeal to consumers, especially to DJs, has played an enormous role in the emergence and evolution of the dance music industry in America, with New York City as its center. The picture that emerges from the rather tight connections between 12-inch vinyl technology and DJ performance technology, DJ technique (spinning, mixing) and style (programming, working, remixing) explains how both the acoustic properties of the 12-inch single as analog medium and the physicality of the equipment (records, turntables, mixers) have helped shape the art and craft of dance music performance as it developed in New York City for more than a quarter of a century. Although during this time other sound carriers were developed and mass-marketed, it is not surprising that most New York DJs, and virtually all those who work in the dance underground prefer vinyl over any other sound carrier format.

Kai Fikentscher, *"You Better Work!": Underground Dance Music in New York City.* Hanover, NH: Wesleyan University Press, 2000.

millionaires. Along with air miles and their celebrity lifestyle, the superstar DJs have also accumulated serious money. It was recently reported that DJ Paul Oakenfold paid £2.7 million for a six-storey, seven-bedroom Regency house in Bayswater.

But the new acid house culture wasn't about DJs at first. If the DJs, even the good ones, weren't quite anonymous, they certainly weren't the stars. Sasha remembers going to the Hacienda in 1988 unaware of who was DJ-ing; uninterested in fact. The first time I met him I was DJ-ing and he came into the DJ box with my friend Zeeba.

I DJ-ed at the Hacienda nearly five hundred times. As the scene grew and other clubs opened and more DJs started playing, you began to realise that some nights were better than others, some DJs were more consistent, some who were great technically but couldn't work a crowd.

Once you've accepted that differences exist between DJs— that some might be more populist and peak time, or some more challenging, or some just plain uncommercial—and once you've witnessed the way the right guest DJ can prompt a queue round the corner and massive attention in the press, then you're acknowledging that every DJ has a market value; hence the inflationary fees the DJs with the right reputations can pick up.

When Sasha was starting out, dance music was buoyant after the emergence of acid house, but the guest DJ, travelling to clubs and playing a set for two or three hours, was still a rarity. Most clubs employed resident DJs who played the full six or seven hours a club was open. But as DJs like Sasha began to have particular crowd-pulling power, clubs round the country wanted a piece of the action. Now house music is a worldwide phenomenon, the circuit is international.

Dance music had fragmented by the mid-1990s; and the mix and range of music that would fill the Hacienda dancefloor when Sasha started going out in the first flush of acid house euphoria was replaced by specialist DJs hosting specialist nights. Genres proliferated. Hardcore rave had its own scene, as did drum & bass, trance, techno, and retro disco.

Travelling, you need to know the kind of club you'll be playing—or, at least, your agent has to be aware—or the consequences can be embarrassing. You hope the promoter is on

top of his game and hasn't booked a load of techno DJs in a soul club, or an underground house DJ in a rave club. You have to match the right DJ to the right audience.

Gilles Peterson is head honcho at the Talkin Loud label and a DJ of great taste, with a regular Monday night at Bar Rumba and one of the best shows on Radio One. The other summer he was booked to play at 'Home' at Space in Ibiza at a gig set up by Radio One (for live broadcast). Due to follow Carl Cox, Gilles had a few reservations about it, but Radio One reassured him; "So I had to go on straight afterwards to 2,000 absolute ravers and live on Radio One," he recalls. "I killed it. It was horrendous really."

At first, the growth in the status of DJs from the early 1990's onwards was partly due to the way that the music press and the record industry need stars of some sort, figureheads, icons; in the face of a flood of records from Detroit and Chicago, many made by anonymous or unknown studio-bound musicians, focus fell on the person digging them out, putting them together. In December 1991 Sasha was *Mixmag* magazine's cover star, with the words 'Sasha the First Pin Up DJ?'.

Subsequently, the rise of the superstar DJs was reinforced by their increased involvement with making records. Hip hop DJs were chopping between key parts of records, creating new sounds, and other DJs were being employed to remix conventional records, beefing up the basslines, re-writing the drum parts, to give the songs club appeal. On the front-line, DJs had developed an instinct for what works on a dancefloor.

Sasha's Unfocussed Career

In 1991, Sasha was a rumour, a DJ only the lucky few had heard or seen—he hadn't even set foot in a recording studio—but by 1994 he was beginning to be known for his records, as an artist. He couldn't DJ everywhere, so his mix CD's, records and remixes took him to a wider audience, although compared to the likes of Fatboy Slim and Paul Van Dyk, Sasha's involvement in music-making has been fitful; one-off singles, remixes, collaborations.

That first bit of front cover stardom ten years ago could have been the peak of Sasha's career, but despite his slightly unfocussed attitudes to his work, he's survived, and somehow still

gives the impression that his best days lie ahead. In 1991 he'd already come a long way from the fish factory, just as club culture has come a long way from dodgy rooms in damp basements. But he'd also got a long way to go; global stardom, more front covers.

Unlike many of the other premier league DJs he has achieved his status without working on radio and without a major record contract. He says he never had a career plan, but here he is, so much in demand, attracting so much devotion, putting one record on after another.

Back at the Arches in Glasgow, the stage—eight big pieces of steel decking—is set up at one end of the venue. Behind the stage, there's a clump of amps and wires and other equipment, and a few people with a backstage view including the promoter—Ricky McGowan—and Erick Morillo, who is due to play a set in the other room later in the evening.

When we arrive with the boxes of records, DJs Craig Richards and Lee Burridge are on, their decks illuminated by a bright green desk light. Either side of them are two semi-spherical mirrorballs which send mini-spots of light spinning round the room. Next to the stage are two banks of speakers, on top of which giant floodlights punch beams into the crowd. Three or four yards from the decks crash barriers have been set up, and the crowd are right up against them. The bulk of the hall is swathed in blue and purple lights. The American girls pass Sasha their coats for safekeeping, Sparrow disappears, and Sasha starts sorting his vinyl again, taking records from each box and putting them in a pile behind the decks, smoking a cigarette. Just before 1.30 he appears at Craig Richards' shoulder, ready to take over, and a big cheer goes up. This is the sharp end of DJ-ing, when the talking and preparations are over. Now it's down to the DJ, his records, and the excitement, the energy contained in the room.

The Artist at Work

Now I'm looking out to see what he can see when he stands at the turntables. Beyond the first few yards, the audience is just a tumult of raised hands, sweaty bodies, silhouettes, and darkness, and at the front staring faces pale with expectation. Someone is onstage with a microphone: "Glasgow, welcome the man

called Sasha!" The lights start strobing, the cheer is massive. Sasha puts on the first record; not some big, banging tune everyone knows, but a quiet, complicated record, just the gentle sounds of tablas.

In our backstage area the American girls start to dance. Sparrow returns with armfuls of Miller Draft. Sasha's drawing out the tension, introducing layers of sound over the rhythms. The beat starts to boom, boom; twisting basslines and snatches of melody bounce around the brick arches. Sasha barely registers the crowd's presence; there are no theatrics. He caresses the records with loose, light movements, a touch on the cross fader, his hands gently flickering over the mixer. He's building, building his set. Out front it's pandemonium.

The Haçienda and the Manchester Scene

Mark O'Donnell

Tony Wilson has been a driving force in the development of dance and rave in the United Kingdom and
America. In the late 1970s, Wilson was the host of
his own pathbreaking music show, "So It Goes," on
Granada TV in England. His Manchester, England,
nightclub, the Haçienda, founded in 1982, was the
most famous dance club in the world throughout the
1980s and was the launching pad of the "Madchester"
house music sound and contemporary rave/dance culture. A related venture, the Factory Records label,
was responsible for bringing such seminal bands as
Joy Division, New Order, and the Happy Mondays
onto the international stage. In the following selection, Mark O'Donnell interviews Wilson about the
Manchester phenomenon, which was the subject of
Michael Winterbottom's 2002 film *24-Hour Party
People*. O'Donnell writes for the "Manchester After
Dark" feature of Manchester.com.

IT'S A TYPICALLY BLUSTERY DAY IN CENTRAL
Manchester as I stroll down to Atlas Bar—a fabulous bar-cum-
eatery that tweaks the nose of the mono-bar culture permeat-
ing most of the city these days. Inside and on home turf I see
the entrepreneur and music industry maverick Tony Wilson.

■

Mark O'Donnell, interview with Tony Wilson, "Manchester After Dark," www.man
chester.com, April 4, 2002. Reproduced by permission of the author. marksubliminal
@hotmail.com.

He is sat with the proprietors discussing a recent remix deal and enjoying a fresh cappuccino. This is a part of town Tony still frequents; Atlas is a firm favourite with meeja [British slang: "media"] types and it has been Tony's stomping ground for many years. Up the road on Whitworth Street of course is the remnants of the Haçienda nightclub. The Haçienda was once the embodiment of a music city on the cutting edge of youth culture; a music city Tony has played a leading role in for the best part of three decades. And it is this role that has been immortalised in film and print with the release of the *24-Hour Party People* movie and Wilson's novelisation of the events.

Before we deal with the film and the book lets take a trip down memory lane.

The Birth of the Manchester Scene

If you spin the wheel of time back to the mid-70's, Wilson cut his teeth as a presenter at Granada TV, after receiving a degree at Cambridge University, and was always on the look out for something fresh and exciting. It has been said about Tony that he 'listens to people, more importantly he has been around the right people to listen to.' Both a visionary and an enthusiast he 'never underestimates the way a culture can appear marginal one year and mainstream the next.'

In 1976 he was invited to attend the Sex Pistols gig at The Free Trade Hall in Manchester; a night put on by Howard Devoto and Pete Shelly who, inspired by what they witnessed, went on to form The Buzzcocks. The first Pistols gig is one of those events that as the mists of time cloud people's memories, many more people claim to have attended than were actually there. In total there was 42 people present, many of whom played a significant role in what was to follow: The Buzzcocks, Peter Hook & Bernard Sumner (Joy Division/New Order), Morrissey, Tony, of course, oh and some ginger nugget called Mick Hucknall.

Invigorated by the show, which was initially bewildering, yet became "deeply and fabulously exciting," Tony premiered the Sex Pistols 'Anarchy In The UK' on his ground breaking Granada TV music show 'So It Goes' in the autumn of 1976. "The thing about the Pistols and punk is you cannot under-

stand it, unless you understand how utterly abysmal popular music in the 70's was," he reflects, cringing at the thought of the chief offenders. "And the Pistols and punk came along and blew it all away."

A do-it-yourself mentality gripped the city. What transpired produced an energy-packed homemade scene fuelled by the bands, by the fanzines and by the people at Manchester's underground clubs. Wilson brought it—with a religious zeal—to the masses on his music show and alongside his original partner Alan Erasmus, designer Peter Saville, the revolutionary producer Martin Hannett and Joy Division's manager Rob Gretton, they released adventurous independent music as Factory Records.

Punk's Child: Joy Division

From the outset the most coveted band in their stable were the dark and mysterious Joy Division.

When questioned about Joy Division's significance, Tony is "eternally grateful to Bernard Sumner (Joy Division/New Order)," for his wise words on a [BBC] Radio One documentary. "I always knew that Joy Division were incredibly important but didn't quite know why," he says peering intently over his glasses. "I am usually quite good at that, being an academic, that's what I am here for," he offers as a casual aside. "Bernard said, 'it (punk) only allowed the expression of a simple emotion. Sooner or later, someone is going to take the simplicity of the instrumentation, the power of its simplicity, its attitude, and express more complex emotions.' Punk would just say f— you! Someone had to use punk and say we are lost—that happened to be Joy Division."

The ripples of the punk explosion resonated for years; sadly, in his prime, Ian Curtis, lead singer of Joy Division, took his own life. The remaining members of the band were later, with the addition of Gillian Gilbert, to form New Order. They became phenomenally popular; the release of 'Blue Monday' remains the biggest selling UK 12" ever, shifting [selling] over three and a half million copies worldwide. This caused one hell of a problem. In the pursuit of aesthetic excellence the art and packaging costs flew sky-high and the infamous Factory record deal ('50/50 profit share, musicians own everything,

artists own right to f— off and Factory pays for publishing costs') meant that every copy sold ended up costing the label 2 pence [about 4¢].

After playing its part in one youth culture explosion, Factory was also immersed in another at the arse end of the 1980's. Acid house was in effect, the lines between rock and dance music were blurring and before long Manchester was popularly coined as 'Madchester' where mad-ferit kids danced freakily, sported huge baggy trousers and adopted the swagger and street suss [smarts] of bands like The Happy Mondays.

The Happy Mondays and Factory's Misery

What set The Mondays apart? "Someone had to take Black American music, add irony and English rock," constructs Wilson. "They did it and everyone f—king copied them," he asserts. "3 months later you get 'Loaded' by Primal Scream and 'Fools Gold' by Stone Roses and everyone is like 'Oh my God the World has changed.' It was the Mondays that did it." Calling on a witness, he cites the *Daily Telegraph:* 'it was the rhythm section: the bass player and the drummer; Paul Ryder and Gary Whelan changed British music forever.'

"Joy Division and New Order are quite rightly considered the top 30 or 40 bands ever and The Mondays aren't—that's wrong. As if somehow, Shaun [Ryder, Happy Mondays' singer/songwriter], hiding behind his genius, writing for the *Daily Sport* and appearing in photos with crap bimbos, detracts from his genius." Not that this affects the belief of his former label boss. "There is no doubt that there are four LP's, a bunch of other songs, and it's one of the greatest collections of pop and rock and roll songs that belong to anyone."

Into the 1990's and the nation high on credit, tightened their purse strings in the face of imminent recession. The property crash wiped millions off the Factory assets and by 1992 it was going under. The Haçienda, awash with gang violence, licensing problems and the first ecstasy related death in a UK nightclub, proved a heavy load. In their most desperate hour Factory needed to release a new album, but the New Order LP was way behind schedule in Ibiza [an island off the coast of Spain]. Meanwhile over in Barbados, The Happy Mondays were breaking limbs, crashing cars and smoking crack cocaine;

all of which (rumour has it) culminated in Ryder getting caught trying to shift [reggae singer] Eddy Grant's recording studio sofas to the local dealers.

Peter Saville once described the life and times of the Factory Records enterprise as "aimless serendipity." Tony, in his book, notes the label was built on "anarchic sentimentalism about the role of popular art," heavily influenced by Situationist [French anticapitalist movement 1957–1972] ideology. Being very honest about the economics of Factory, he states, "we were hardly astute business men."

The End of Factory and the Haçienda

Even though the Haçienda inevitably shut its doors, its legend was secured. It was a fortress for acid house (using the DJ as the medium) and a precursor for the dance music super club. "What made the Hacienda so special was the Gothic Cathedral type space, made so your prayers and emotions are rising up to heaven," says Wilson. "For the celebratory act of dance music it was perfect." Unfortunately it never made any money. "We didn't sell E [Ecstasy] at the bar," is Tony's logic.

I put forward the notion that there were other forces at work that contributed to the demise of the Haçienda. "It would be nice to blame others," he replies, "and there is no doubt that the Greater Manchester Police behaved very badly. The idea of closing a venue that gangsters go to would resolve the problem—which was their clear strategy in the early 90's—is brainless. The real nail in the coffin was the changing of bar licensing hours to 2am. That destroyed clubbing in Manchester and destroyed the Haçienda. We all had clubs and bars and thought what a great idea to make our city more cosmopolitan. We thought we are now a 24-hour city, fantastic. About two weeks later we knew we had f—ed up."

The DJ as Artist

Bill Brewster and Frank Broughton

Bill Brewster and Frank Broughton, both former editors of *Mixmag's Update USA*, trace the history of the disk jockey from the late 1970s to the early 1990s. Brewster and Broughton focus particular attention on how late-twentieth-century DJ culture developed in the United Kingdom as part of a feedback loop between the British and American DJs who were electrifying clubs on both sides of the Atlantic. The authors also reflect on the unlikely ascendance of DJs, who have transformed from humble spinners of other people's music into music producers and creators in their own right who can pack the clubs with their marquee star power.

THE DJ'S CRAFT AND HIS SKILLS WERE CLOSE TO fully formed as long as twenty years ago. Disco and hip hop were his moments of true innovation. Most advances since then have come in his role as a producer, and in his possession of a good manager. But with wily representation and clever marketing, the DJ is now the hero of his age, a popstar, a crowd-draw, a reliable brand name. And he gets paid (like supermodels and movie stars, those other victors of late consumer capitalism) not according to how talented he is, nor how hard he works, but by the size of his franchise—how many ears he can reach and how many units he can shift.

How did all this happen?

The Arrival

The first explosion was loud, alien, devastating. It was the sound, between 1979 and '82, of hip hop announcing its British

■

Bill Brewster and Frank Broughton, *Last Night a DJ Saved My Life*. New York: Grove Press, 2000. Copyright © 1999 by Bill Brewster and Frank Broughton. Reproduced by permission of Grove/Atlantic for North America and Headline for the rest of the world rights.

arrival: "Rappers' Delight," "Flash's Adventures On The Wheels Of Steel," Kurtis Blow, Tanya Winley, Funky Four (Plus One More), "Planet Rock.". . .

Matt Black of Coldcut, DJ and UK house pioneer, was hit square in the chest by the blast: "It just blew apart conceptions of what a song should be like. It was so far out, so radical."

"Everyone was completely like . . . 'Oh my god, what *is* this?'" recalls Dave Dorrell, DJ and another early UK house producer. "Rap, hip hop, was way beyond anything that you were accustomed to, or able to comprehend. It was a foreign language. What are these people doing? How do they do this? And what would it be like to see them doing it? It had just arrived here, and it was causing mayhem. Devastation. All of a sudden it was like, 'How can we get more of this drug?'"

The second impact, a few years later in 1985, '86, '87, came from house. Another alien musical language, equally devastating—Morse code from Mars. . . .

"House just had a phenomenal impact," says Black. "Even straight away you realized that here was a new kind of music. As soon as you heard it you realized that here was a new form of energy that had materialized.". . .

The Soul Mafia

At the beginning of the eighties, despite a healthy underground club culture, the British DJ lagged far behind his American counterpart. While the leading disco DJs in New York were already moving into production and remixing, in the UK the successful DJ was either a "personality" who chatted inanely between records, or a connoisseur who collected, appreciated and evangelized. The postdisco sounds of hip hop and house would soon revolutionize their craft, but before these new genres arrived, British DJs were largely unaware of the creative possibilities that disco had unleashed.

Even basic mixing techniques, *de rigueur* in New York since the start of the seventies, didn't make it over to the UK until 1978, when an American DJ called Greg James was imported to show how it was done. Brought over to play at London's newly refurbished Embassy Club, James stayed in England for several years and schooled many young DJs, including Jazzy M, in American techniques (as well as running the Spin-Offs record store in west London).

There were several strong dance scenes existing at this time. The "Soul Mafia" was a small clique of soul and funk DJs centered around Chris Hill and Robbie Vincent. Younger mafiosi included Johnny Walker and Pete Tong, as well as Froggy, another of the DJs to whom Greg James had passed on his skills. Chris Hill had built a considerable reputation from the mid-seventies by playing a strong selection of hard-to-find black American imports first at the Goldmine in Canvey Island, and then the Lacey Lady in Ilford (both satellite towns to the east of London). . . .

The Soul Mafia coalesced around Hill's success. Its following was resolutely suburban and largely white. Here was a scene that elevated the smooth boogie of Kleeer and the bland soul of Maze to mythic status. Its dancefloors were usually filled with boys wearing alarmingly tight shorts, deck shoes and singlets, often brandishing cannon-sized air-horns. Although there were plenty of girls there, it was still a male-oriented scene. Initially no club owners would give up their prime weekend spots to them so the Soul Mafia's strength derived largely from all-dayers and Sunday events (like the "speed garage" scene years later). The all-dayers often attracted renegade northern soul fans who, despite the two scenes' considerable musical differences, would travel down to dance alongside the southern jazz-funkers. North also met south at soul weekenders like Caister and Bognor Regis, and all-dayers at Bournemouth, Birmingham and Leeds, where progressive northern jocks like Colin Curtis and Jonathan Woodliffe found common purpose with Chris Hill and with London DJs like Jay Strongman and Paul Anderson.

In the south underground club culture was fairly limited at this time so the Soul Mafia's influence was substantial. However, hip hop's arrival greatly eroded any notion of musical consensus and by 1987 there were massive fissures in the scene. . . .

Rare Groove and the Warehouse Scene

Another significant UK scene through the eighties was to be found among the crumbling concrete of inner city London. Here imported Jamaican sound system culture had been put to fresh use by second-generation West Indians like Jazzie B, Norman and Joey Jay and Derek B. Inspired by club DJs George Power, Mark Roman and Greg Edwards, they largely

eschewed their parents' dub and reggae tastes in favor of a grittier, more urban soundtrack. This mixed funk and soul together with the dramatic new U.S. import, hip hop, to make music perfectly suited to kids raised in the shadows of gloomy W11 tower blocks. Having been excluded from many west end clubs because of racist door policies, black kids found their entertainment in sound systems like Soul II Soul, Shake'n'fingerpop, Hard Rock, Funkadelic and Good Groove.

The sound crystallized around Norman Jay's "The Original Rare Groove Show" on Kiss FM—then a pirate station—where Jay reintroduced seventies funk tracks to an attentive audience. Although the warehouse scene was never wholly about such records (go-go, hip hop, electro and even early house were as likely to feature in its playlists), these were quickly used as a journalistic shorthand, and the music was dubbed "rare groove," after Jay's show.

As a largely retro form, rare groove picked up many of the same characteristics as northern soul. DJs searched rabidly for obscurities, paid huge sums for them and covered up labels to protect their identities. However, the fact that it was based resolutely in urban London gave it far greater cachet than the northern scene had ever enjoyed. Record companies leapt on it as a trendy way to market back catalogue material, its racially-mixed crowd and their funky seventies fashions were celebrated in the new "style" magazines, *i-D* and *The Face*, and rare groove grew into a fairly influential cultural force. And it was far from the whole story. There were weekend-long punk parties in docklands, the more unorthodox dance modes of Dirtbox and the chi-chi extravagance of Westworld's big-ticket parties. The presence of such a vibrant nightlife, enjoying the patronage of the capital's tastemakers, was the main factor delaying the acceptance of house in London.

"There wasn't really a need to change," remembers DJ/producer Terry Farley. "Everyone was running around wearing Duffer and flares, Norman Jay was carrying the swing with Gilles Peterson and the Young Disciples. There were great parties going on. Norman Jay did a Shake'n'fingerpop at the Town & Country Club in 1987 and there were 4,000 people in there. You'd go to a club and Bobby Byrd would be playing. It was brilliant. London was really, really happening in '87."

Eventually, as we'll see, the warehouse scene and many of its DJs would form a foundation for the acid house explosion, giving it the underground structures—unlicensed venues and an effective communications network—by which it would establish itself. However, for a long time rare groove prevented house gaining a foothold.

The Haçienda and Madchester

While the south was violently divided over house, the north had no such hesitancy. DJs Graeme Park at Nottingham's Garage and Mike Pickering at Manchester's Haçienda fell for it wholesale, as did their clubbers.

"They were more on it," says Pete Tong. "The day a house record came in, they chucked all the old ones out. They were looking at us, going, 'You f—ing southern soul tossers!'"

The Haçienda was opened on May 21, 1982 by stone-age funnyman Bernard Manning. His famously bigoted jokes didn't go down too well and he returned his fee, saying, "Take my advice, never hire a comedian." The forward-looking musical policy was also a little out of sync with the clientele's expectations. The original resident DJ, Hewan Clark, programmed a mix of black funk, soul and disco, while sullen students mooched around the cavernous space in raincoats waiting in vain for Echo & the Bunnymen to be played.

The club was the brainchild of a group of Manchester music folk including Tony Wilson, supremo of Factory Records, and Rob Gretton, New Order's manager. It even had a Factory catalogue number, HAÇ 51. And it was modeled unashamedly on the great clubs of New York: the Paradise Garage and Danceteria. As Wilson put it: "I just thought, why hasn't Manchester got one of those? F—ing New York's got one, we should have one."

New Order were also among the club's directors, and as the band was regularly over in New York recording with Arthur Baker, they formed the lynchpin of the Manc-yank connection. "There's always been this big underground link with New York, because of New Order and Factory's early success there," Mike Pickering told Jon Savage in *The Haçienda Must Be Built*. "The most important thing about the [New York club] Paradise Garage was that Larry Levan used to mix

these underground New York records with records on [British labels] Rough Trade or Factory, and that was what first got me really into New York. As far as I was concerned, the dream was that the Haçienda would be like that."

As well as these connections to New York's more progressive clubs, the scene in the north of England could claim close musical kinship with Chicago and Detroit. Northern soul had made earlier ties and, more recently, electronic bands from England's northern industrial cities—Human League, Cabaret Voltaire, ABC, New Order—had provided crucial inspiration for the pioneers of house and techno. The "new romantic" movement, as this became known, is nowadays derided for its chronic narcissism and overuse of Max Factor [a brand of makeup] but many of its records still stand as darkly electronic slices of futurism. . . .

The Revolution Will Be Synthesized

Upon arrival in the UK, hip hop and then house did far more than just divide people along lines of taste. With them these new forms also brought radically new ways of making music. They brought amazing new ways of even *thinking* about music. Hip hop fostered the idea of sampling, of stealing rather than emulating, of making patchwork music from a multitude of sources. House encouraged this idea too, and house also showed—quite conclusively—that music made with drum machines and synthesizers could be as sexy, funky and downright danceable as anything made with wood, brass and steel.

Now, given that these new postdisco forms had been created by DJs, it was no surprise that DJs were best placed to adopt them. House and hip hop had both emerged as the DJ's response to the demands of his dancefloor, they were based on the DJ's peculiar understanding of music, and they were made in ways that most DJs could easily follow. House and hip hop were revolutionary for the jolt of novelty and excitement they gave the UK club scene, but they were also vitally significant because they made the DJ's move to production inevitable. With rare groove ruling the roost there was little pressure to venture into the studio: unless he was also a talented musician or experienced producer, a DJ in love with old soul records or polished jazz-funk didn't have much hope of making his own

music. However, a DJ blown over by the sound collages of hip hop or energized by the synthetic beats of house might perfectly well expect to cook some up for himself. A generation of British DJs became remixers and producers as a result, and in the ever-fertile musical melting pot of urban Britain, a new era of dance music began. . . .

DJ/Producer/Remixer

New technology was a vital force in Britain, as it had been in Chicago and Detroit. When the first wave of UK house broke, affordable digital sampling was yet to come, but tape sampling was easy enough and drum machines and synthesizers were becoming ever more commonplace. With these digital instruments, the punk manifesto that anyone could make music, no-experience-necessary, could be fully realized. Visionary composer John Cage had once written, "What we can't do ourselves will be done by machines and electrical instruments which we will invent." Now such machines were a reality and would-be producers were able to sidestep the fact that they had zero musical training (and sidestep studio fees of £1,000 [about $2,000 U.S.] a day) and immediately start putting music together in their bedrooms.

DJ/producer Norman Cook, then playing bass with the Housemartins, agrees that the punk do-it-yourself ethos was important: "There was an irreverence to the rules, like you can make a record that's really repetitive and isn't very musical and was made at home in your bedroom and doesn't have chords, drummers, singers, or anyone who can read a musical note.". . .

Since the DJ is an expert at making people dance, it was inevitable that he would eventually dominate the making of dance music itself. Most successful DJs now carry the job title DJ/producer/remixer. Making their own records, or reconstructing those made by others, is a natural extension of the club DJ's trade, a way to put his creative stamp on the world. It's a way of distilling the particular sound he favors in his club performances into a more tangible form and, importantly, it's how a DJ can most convincingly claim artist status.

"Most DJs become DJs because they love the music, and if you love the music, you feel you have some of it in you waiting to come out," says Norman Cook. "You're playing tracks

that are really simple. You think, this is just a couple of samples and a drum machine, I bet I could probably do that. And invariably, you can."

The DJ has a powerful advantage when it comes to making music digitally. Today, thanks to the (DJ-derived) concept of musical collage and the equipment which makes it possible, what a producer does in the studio to make a dance record is almost identical to what he would do to make a remix, and little different in principle from what a DJ does in a club. When a good DJ performs, he will be layering parts of records over each other, introducing snatches of one into a second, weaving and splicing different elements to make an original suite of music. Similarly, making or remixing a dance record is usually a case of playing around with relatively large chunks of sound (i.e., samples and predetermined rhythms), and combining them to make something new. The studio allows much greater levels of complexity, but at heart, constructing or reconstructing a dance record is very like a compressed version of DJing in a club.

The new methodology has the added bonus of being technically undemanding. With a good studio engineer to actually press all the buttons and achieve the desired results, it's perfectly possible for a complete novice to make a great dance record. All they need are workable musical ideas. And a good DJ, even the most technically clueless, will have a steady supply of those.

"When you're DJing, you spend untold hours just standing watching people dance," explains Cook. "And you begin to realize which bits of a record people react to and which bits get them going. You just learn what makes people dance." And this experience translates easily into inspiration for remixing and production. "When I'm in the studio, I think back to the night before and what kind of things worked with dancers. You remember how you felt when you put a tune on and it rocked the crowd; or when you played a groove that the crowd totally got into, even when they'd never heard the record before. It doesn't necessarily mean you make great pop music, but if your music's aimed straight at the dancefloor it gives you a head start."

Most DJs would agree that the leap from playing records to making them is a small one; few see the move from DJ

booth to recording studio as anything other than a natural progression. "Everything I've learned is through playing records. It triggered everything," says Kenny "Dope" Gonzales, one half of Nuyorican duo Masters At Work, one of the most respected remix/production teams of the nineties. "DJing was our training and it still is," adds his partner "Little" Louie Vega. "Learning the structure of songs, the bars, the breaks, is all through DJing."

The Evolution of the Remix

Remixing was first done in Jamaica in the sixties when DJ/producers started to unravel songs into one-off versions and dubplates, making them more effective for outdoor sound systems. A similar goal was at work in mid seventies New York when the disco and hip hop DJs started the technique of cutting rapidly from one record to another to extend the best passages, and began reconstructing songs on reel-to-reel for the same effect. Many of the disco DJs enjoyed careers as commercial remixers and in New York at least it was quickly an accepted part of the job—a way for the DJ to feed his dancefloor, to make his performance more distinctive and, by making nondancey songs suitable for a dancefloor, to enlarge his armory of records.

Remixing, at its simplest, is usually a straightforward process of sorting out a track's good elements from bad, relative to the dancefloor. As Paul Oakenfold puts it "Someone'll play you something. You say, 'That's wrong, that's wrong, that's wrong,' take all of them out and replace them with this, this, this and this. Rearrange it—and it'll work."

This basic description belies the fact that the concept of the remix has evolved dramatically. A remix can be anything from a slightly different arrangement of a song to a track that bears hardly any relation to the original.

At first the remixer only made structural changes. Record companies were very protective of the original song and it was all you could do to add a conga.

"In the beginning, you remixed the original track," explains David Morales, one of the world's best-known remixers. "You used what was there to create the intro, your body, your break, your tag—the end of the song."

But remixers were soon allowed to add a few new elements.

"You might change the bassline, add percussion, or you added some other things, but you still had the song. You still had the artist intact."

A third stage came when the vocal track was used intact but the music accompanying it was replaced completely. "You started to put *new* music on remixes. And all you had left from the original was the vocal track. Now people expected to hear something totally different when they bought a remix."

Finally, remixers were given a free hand to scrap anything from the original and add anything they liked from other sources. In some, nothing of the original record remained except perhaps a tiny sampled snatch of vocals or instrumentation. Here, the remixer constructed an entirely new track and incorporated a few yelps from the singer, or a couple of stabs from a guitar. Strictly speaking, the remixer was now doing full production (although not getting any royalties or publishing fees for it, because contractually it was almost always only a remix). This is today's most common form of remixing. "It's totally leftfield now," says Morales. "It's totally in another place. I mean, let's not even call it remixing anymore. It's production."

Now that such radical remixing is so prevalent, the success of a dance record often has very little to do with the original artist or the original song. To a craftsman like Morales who prides himself on respecting the original, and who is one of a select few who are capable of full vocal remixes, this is overstepping the mark.

"Somebody says, 'I need a remix.' So you take a piece of a vocal: '*Bla*' and stick it on a rhythm track you have already sitting around. That's a remix? That represents the artist? That doesn't represent the artist, it represents *you*."

But for many an ambitious DJ/remixer, that is the whole point.

Remix and Restyle

Take a painting, cut it into pieces and rearrange the bits. How much do you have to change it before the end result is your work and no longer something made by someone else? Does it help if more people like your collage than liked the original painting? Can the collage be a genuinely new piece of art?

By the end of the seventies, DJs knew that the remix could

go further than just make a song more *functional* for the dance-floor. It also offered them a route into the record industry and the means to finally gain recognition as creative artists. By adding stylistic twists, they could give a song the precise musical flavor they wanted, and if their enhancements were individual enough, these would mark out the remixer—rather than the original writer/musician—as the creative force behind a track. If their particular flavor was reasonably consistent over a series of records, a remixer could even develop a "sound," just like any other recording artist. And since a DJ's remixes were usually based on the kind of music he chose to play when he performed in a club, the musical style evident on his remixes would serve to reinforce and further distinguish the musical style of his DJing, and vice versa. Through remixing, the DJ had a way of pushing his music in a distinctive direction, both on the dancefloor and in the studio.

When remixes started being more successful than their originals (usually because they'd been made infinitely more danceable), the remixers started taking the limelight away from the original artists. And as remixes strayed further and further away from their originals stylistically, they started to look like completely new things. The new studio methods had made remixing and production more or less indistinguishable, as had the hip hop DJs who had started producing records by more or less recreating their live performance in the studio. By the mid-eighties, certain remixers were enjoying name recognition and both dancefloor and chart success, and as the DJ's new postdisco genres took hold, the lines between remixing and authorship started to fade.

The idea that a remixer can make something new, that he can do something as creative as original production, has its earliest precedent in Jamaica. Here, since the sixties, certain dub remixers had enjoyed equal recognition to the artists in their records. However, it took a while before this idea gained currency anywhere else. Disco produced several star remixers—pioneers like Tom Moulton, Walter Gibbons, Jim Burgess—but they never enjoyed star billing on their records: appreciation of their artistry was largely confined to the closed world of other DJs. Slightly later, figures such as Shep Pettibone, Jellybean, Larry Levan and François Kevorkian were recognized as hav-

ing a magic touch, and often when they did a remix their names were fairly prominent on the credits. However, when Epic in the UK emphasized Kevorkian's name above all others on a compilation of his disco remixes, his U.S. label Prelude was incensed that the remixer's name should overshadow the acts themselves.

Genuinely Creative Activity

It was really only with the emergence of house that remixing was widely seen as a genuinely creative activity, when the key DJs of the period—Frankie Knuckles, David Morales, Tony Humphries—made having a reputation as a DJ and a reputation as a dance producer/remixer virtually interchangeable. A DJ's studio work started to become, as it is today, an important means of self-promotion and in the UK at least, the DJ/remixer had started his journey towards pop-star status.

Certain American jocks became gods in the UK, not by virtue of their DJ performances, but simply because of their studio work. Brooklyn producer/remixer Todd Terry exemplified this. In the middle of the nineties he commanded a DJ fee higher than anybody, yet his fame came not from playing records but from production and remixing. And his success in this came from marking himself out with a highly distinctive style. By grafting the hard New York hip hop aesthetic onto house, he had brought a richer, stronger percussion palette to the genre in records like Royal House's "Can You Party" and Todd Terry Project's "Weekend" and "Bango" (all 1988). "That Chicago sound. I took it to the next level," he says. "You'd listen to it and say only Todd would do that, that's Todd's drum pattern, that's his *sound*, the dark, wild hype sound."

By 1990 the wider music industry felt ready to invest in the idea of the DJ as artist, and there was a signing frenzy in which Frankie Knuckles, Blaze, Robert Clivilles and David Cole, and Lil Louis were all awarded album contracts. On the whole they were marketed as producers who happened to be DJs, with different vocalists and musicians appearing on each track. But most of these album projects bombed commercially (only Clivilles and Cole, as C&C Music Factory, enjoyed any real success) and U.S. major labels once again saw dance music as a risky business, and the idea of the DJ as recording artist as

something best left to the independents.

The DJ's rise to artist status was finally ratified in 1993, when a DJ's remix album was released with all the fanfare of a major artist and aimed, in the wake of the UK's dance transformation, squarely at the pop market. Sasha (Alexander Coe), a DJ who had risen to fame as resident at Shelley's, a club in the north of England, released an album made up entirely of remixes (*Sasha: The Remixes*). These weren't songs that he had originated in the studio. He wasn't presented as a producer who was incidentally also a DJ. These were songs originally written and recorded by other artists entirely, and many of them well-known, successful artists. Sasha had only *remixed* the tracks. Despite this, these reconstructions were on *his* album, with *his* name in the title, and were to be considered *his* pieces of music. But most importantly, unlike the two or three remix albums that had predated it, it wasn't a small pressing aimed strictly at connoisseurs and other DJs. It was a major release. "Sasha is living proof of the dictum that DJs, as dance music's prime movers, are ideally placed to take that music to new levels as producers," declared Nick Gordon Brown's liner notes. "The lines between DJs and artists, remixers and producers are getting ever more blurred."

Detroit Techno, Chicago House, and New York Garage

Simon Reynolds

In the following selection, excerpted from his book *Generation Ecstasy*, Simon Reynolds chronicles the spread of postdisco, 1980s-era electronic dance music as it emigrated from Detroit to Germany and back to the United States, where American DJs transformed the skittering beats of "Krautrock" into the three signature styles of American electronic dance music. These styles—techno, house, and garage—were in fact microcultural movements that crystallized around the three American urban epicenters (Detroit, Chicago, and New York, respectively) of rave's first decade.

Simon Reynolds is a senior editor at *Spin* magazine whose work has appeared in the *New York Times*, *Rolling Stone*, and *Details*, to name but a few publications. Reynolds maintains a Web site and weblog, "Simon Sez: A White Brit Rave Aesthete Thinks Aloud," which can be accessed at http://members.aol.com/blissout.

THE STORY OF TECHNO BEGINS NOT IN EARLY-eighties Detroit, as is so often claimed, but in early-seventies Düsseldorf, where Kraftwerk built their KlingKlang sound

∎

Simon Reynolds, *Generation Ecstasy: Into the World of Techno and Rave Culture*. Boston: Little, Brown, 1998. Copyright © 1998 by Simon Reynolds. All rights reserved. Reproduced by permission.

factory and churned out pioneering synth-and-drum-machine tracks like "Autobahn," "Trans-Europe Express," and "The Man-Machine."

In one of those weird pop-historical loops, Kraftwerk were themselves influenced by Detroit—by the adrenalized insurgency of the MC5 and the Stooges (whose noise, Iggy Pop has said, was partly inspired by the pounding clangor of the Motor City's auto factories). Like the other Krautrock bands—Can, Faust, Neu!—Kraftwerk were also inspired by the mantric minimalism and non–R&B rhythms of the Velvet Underground (whose John Cale produced the first Stooges album). Replacing guitars and drums with synthesizer pulses and programmed beats, Kraftwerk sublimated the Velvets' white light/white heat speed rush into the cruise-control serenity of *motorik*, a metronomic, regular-as-carburetor rhythm that was at once post-rock and proto-techno. "Autobahn"—a twenty-four-minute hymn to the exhilaration of gliding down the freeway that sounded like a cyborg Beach Boys—was (in abbreviated form) a chart smash throughout the world in 1975. Two years later on the *Trans-Europe Express* album, the title track—all indefatigable girder beats and arching, Doppler effect synths—segues into "Metal on Metal," a funky iron foundry that sounded like a Luigi Russolo Art of Noises megamix for a futurist discotheque.

"They were so stiff, they were funky," techno pioneer Carl Craig has said of Kraftwerk. This paradox—which effectively translates as "they were so white, they were black"—is as close as anyone has got to explaining the mystery of why Kraftwerk's music had such a massive impact on black American youth. In New York, the German band almost single-handedly sired the electro movement: Afrika Bambaataa and Soulsonic Force's 1982 smash "Planet Rock" stole its doomy melody from "Trans-Europe Express" and its beatbox rhythm from Kraftwerk's 1981 track "Numbers." But while New York hip-hop soon abandoned electro's drum machines for seventies funk breakbeats, Kraftwerk had a more enduring impact in Detroit. Their music's Teutonic rigor and glacial grandeur plugged into the Europhile tastes of arty middle-class black youth and fired the imaginations of three high school friends—Juan Atkins, Derrick May, and Kevin Saunderson—who together invented Detroit

techno. From Cybotron's 1982 "Cosmic Cars" to Carl Craig's 1995 *Autobahn* homage *Landcruising*, the Detroit sound still fits May's famous description: "like [funk musician] George Clinton and Kraftwerk stuck in an elevator with only a sequencer to keep them company."

Techno: The Unlikely Offspring of Germany and Detroit

"When I first heard synthesizers dropped on records it was great . . . like UFOs landing on records, so I got one," Juan Atkins has said. "It wasn't any one particular group that turned me on to synthesizers, but 'Flashlight' [Parliament's number one R&B hit from early 1978] was the first record I heard where maybe 75 percent of the production was electronic."

Atkins was then a sixteen-year-old living in Belleville, a small town thirty miles from Detroit, and playing bass, drums, and "a little bit of lead guitar" in various garage funk bands. He had befriended Derrick May and Kevin Saunderson three years earlier. "In Belleville," remembers Saunderson, "it was pretty racial still at that time, there wasn't a lot of black people there. So we three kind of gelled right away." Atkins became May's musical mentor, hipping him to all kinds of weird shit— Parliament-Funkadelic, Kraftwerk, Gary Numan, Giorgio Moroder, even quirky American New Wave like the B-52's.

Although the music they were into was all dance floor ori- ented, the "Belleville Three"—as Atkins, May, and Saunder- son were later to be mythologized—brought an art-rock seri- ousness to bear on what rock fans then dissed as mere "disco." "For us, it was always a dedication," says May. "We used to sit back and philosophize on what these people thought about when they made their music, and how they felt the next phase of the music would go. And you know, half the shit we thought about the artist never even f—ing thought about! . . . Because Belleville was a rural town, we perceived the music differently than you would if you encountered it in dance clubs. We'd sit back with the lights off and listen to records by Bootsy and Yellow Magic Orchestra. We never just took it as entertain- ment, we took it as a serious philosophy."

The Belleville Three belonged to a new generation of Detroit-area black youth who grew up accustomed to affluence,

thanks in part to the racially integrated United Auto Workers union. "My grandfather worked at Ford for twenty years, he was like a career auto worker," says Atkins. "A lot of the kids that came up after this integration, they got used to a better way of living. If you had a job at the plant at this time, you were making bucks. And it wasn't like the white guy standing next to you is getting five or ten dollars an hour more than you. Everybody was equal. So what happened is that you've got this environment with kids that come up somewhat snobby, 'cos hey, their parents are making money working at Ford or GM or Chrysler, been elevated to a foreman, maybe even to a white-collar job." The Europhilia of these middle-class black youths, says Atkins, was part of their attempt "to distance themselves from the kids that were coming up in the projects, the ghetto.". . .

One expression of this upwardly mobile subculture was clubs and dance music. These weren't nightclubs but high school social clubs with names like Snobs, Brats, Ciabattino, Rafael, and Charivari, who would hire spaces and throw parties. Charivari was named after a New York clothing store and is said to have recorded the first Detroit techno track, titled "Shari Vari," just to play at its own parties. The social club kids were "obsessed with Italian 'progressive' music—Italian disco, basically," says Carl Craig, another early acolyte of May and Atkins. Dubbed "progressive" because their music stemmed from Giorgio Moroder's synth-and-drum-machine-based Eurodisco, rather than the symphonic Philly sound, Italian artists like Alexander Robotnik, Klein and MBO and Capricorn filled the gap left by the death of disco in America. On the Detroit dance party circuit, you would also hear electro-funk from New York labels like West End and Prelude, English New Romantic and Euro-synthpop artists like Visage, Yello, and Telex, and American New Wave from Devo and Talking Heads. "Man, I don't know if this could happen nowhere else in the country but Detroit," laughs Atkins. "Can you imagine three or four hundred black kids dancing to the B-52's' 'Rock Lobster'?". . .

Insane Mixing

Around 1980, Atkins and May started making tentative steps toward becoming DJs themselves. "Juan and I started messing around with the idea of doing our own personal remixes, as a

joke, using a pause button, a tape deck, and a basic turntable. Just taking a record and pausing it up, doing edits with the pause button. We got damn good at it. . . .

May and Atkins applied the same kind of theoretical intensity to the art of mixing and set building that they'd once invested in listening to records. "We built a philosophy behind spinning records. We'd sit and think what the guy who made the record was thinking about, and find a record that would fit with it, so that the people on the dance floor would comprehend the concept. When I think about all the brainpower that went into it! We'd sit up the whole night before the party, think about what we'd play the following night, the people who'd be at the party, the concept of the clientele. It was insane!"

Eventually, the social club party scene got so successful that the *GQ* kids found that an undesirable element began to turn up: the very ghetto youth from the projects that they'd put so much energy into defining themselves against. That was when the clubs started putting the phrase "no jits" on the flyers—"jit" being short for "jitterbug," Detroit slang for gangsta.

"They would put 'no jits allowed,'" says May, "but how you gonna tell some 250-pound ruffneck, standing about six foot four, 'you're not coming to my party'—when you're some little five foot two pretty boy? I don't think so! He's coming in! It was a *hope* that they wouldn't come! It was to make them feel unwanted. . . . West Side kids and the whole elite high school scene just wanted to keep this shit to themselves. . . . It was the beginning of the end. That's when the guns started popping up at the parties, and fights started happening. By '86, it was over.". . .

From Detroit to Chicago

Detroit techno came to the world's attention indirectly, as an adjunct to Chicago's house scene. When British A & R scouts came to Chicago to investigate house music in 1986–87, they discovered that many of the top-selling tracks were actually from Detroit. "We would sell ten to fifteen thousand records in Chicago alone," says Juan Atkins. "We were selling more records in Chicago than even Chicago artists. We kind of went hand in hand with the house movement.

"Chicago was one of a couple of cities in America where disco never died," Atkins continues. "The DJs kept playing it

on radio and in the clubs. And since there were no new disco records coming through they were looking to fill the gap with whatever they could find." This meant Euro synth pop, Italian "progressive," and eventually the early Detroit tracks. The Belleville Three quickly got to know everybody in the Chicago scene. . . .

Despite its Europhile tendencies, Detroit was always more of a funk city than a disco town. This difference came through in the music: the rhythm programming in Detroit techno was more syncopated, had more of a groove. House was propelled by a metronomic, four-to-the-floor beat, what Eddie Fowlkes calls "a straight straight foot"—a reference to the mechanical kick drum that Chicago DJs like Farley "Jackmaster" Funk and Frankie Knuckles would superimpose over their disco mixes. Where Chicago house tended to feature disco-style diva vocals, Detroit tracks were almost always instrumentals. The final difference was that Detroit techno, while arty and upwardly mobile, was a straight black scene. Chicago house was a gay black scene. . . .

In 1987, [rap group] Public Enemy's Chuck D articulated hip-hop's antipathy to house, disco's descendant, declaring: "it's sophisticated, anti-black, anti-feel, the most *artificial* shit I ever heard. It represents the gay scene, it's separating blacks from their past and their culture, it's upwardly mobile."

Music of Double Exclusion

Chicago house music was born of a double exclusion, then: not just black, but gay and black. Its cultural dissidence involved embracing a music that the majority culture deemed dead and buried. House didn't just resurrect disco, it intensified the very aspects that most offended the discophobes: the mechanistic repetition, the synthetic and electronic textures, the rootlessness, the "depraved" hypersexuality and "decadent" drugginess. Stylistically, house assembled itself from disregarded and degraded pop-culture detritus that the mainstream considered passé, disposable, un-American: the proto-disco of the Salsoul and Philadelphia International labels, English synth-pop, and Moroder's Eurodisco. . . .

In the absence of fresh disco product, Chicago DJs had to rework the existing material into new shapes. House—a term

that originally referred to the kind of music you'd hear at the Warehouse, a gay nightclub in Chicago—was born not as a distinct genre but as an approach to making "dead" music come alive, by cut 'n' mix, segue, montage, and other DJ tricks. Just as the term disco derived from the discotheque (a place where you heard recorded music, not live performances), house began as a disc jockey culture. In fact, it was an imported DJ culture, transplanted from New York by Frankie Knuckles, who DJ-ed at the Warehouse from 1979 until 1983. . . .

Intense Competition

With other regular parties emerging, competition between DJs grew fierce. To get an edge over their rivals, DJs would devise more complicated mixing tricks and employ special effects, like Frankie Knuckles's steam locomotive sound. Both Farley and Knuckles started to use a live drum machine to bolster their mixes and make the experience more hypnotic. The stomping four-to-the-floor kick drum would become the defining mark of house music. Other elements—hissing hi-hat patterns, synthetic hand-claps, synth vamps, chiming bass loops, drumrolls that pushed the track to the next plateau of preorgasmic intensity—emerged when Chicagoans started making records to slake the DJs' insatiable demand for fresh material. Called "tracks" as opposed to songs, because they consisted of little more than a drum track, this proto-house music was initially played by DJs on reel-to-reel tape and cassette.

Although many have claimed the title of "first house track," most agree that the first vinyl release was Jesse Saunders and Vince Lawrence's "On and On" (a raw, ultraminimal version of the Salsoul classic by First Choice), which the duo put out in 1983. Saunders and Lawrence approached Larry Sherman, a local entrepreneur who had bought out Chicago's only record-pressing plant, and asked him to press up five hundred 12-inches for them on trust. They promised to return within twenty minutes and pay him $4 per disc. Not only did they come back and pay him in full, they also asked him to press another thousand copies.

Stunned by the demand for this new music in Chicago, Sherman started the Trax label and debuted with another Jesse Saunders track, "Wanna Dance," released under the name Le

Noiz. Sherman's role in the genesis of house is much disputed. Some regard him as a visionary entrepreneur who fostered the scene and provided work for the musicians in the day-to-day operations of Trax. Others accuse Sherman of pursuing short-term profit and neglecting the long-term career prospects of their artists, thereby contributing to the premature demise of the Chicago scene in the late eighties. . . .

The Producer Becomes the Star

House makes the producer, not the singer, the star. It's the culmination of an unwritten (because unwritable) history of black dance pop, a history determined not by sacred cow auteurs but by producers, session musicians, and engineers—backroom boys. House music takes this depersonalization further: it gets rid of human musicians (the house band that gave Motown or Stax or Studio One its distinctive sound), leaving just the producer and his machines. Operating as a cottage factory churning out a high turnover of tracks, the house producer replaces the artist's signature with the industrialist's trademark. Closer to an architect or draftsman, the house auteur is absent from his own creation; house tracks are less like artworks, in the expressive sense, than vehicles, rhythmic engines that take the dancer on a ride.

As well as being post-biographical, house is post-geographical pop. If Chicago is the origin, it's because it happens to be a junction point in the international trade routes of disco. Breaking with the traditional horticultural language we use to describe the evolution of pop—cross-pollination, hybridization—house's "roots" lie in deracination. The music sounds inorganic: machines talking to each other in an unreal acoustic space. When sounds from real-world acoustic sources enter house's pleasuredome, they tend to be processed and disembodied—as with the distortion and manipulation inflicted on the human voice, evacuating its soul and reducing it to a shallow *effect*.

But this is only one side of house culture. Just as important was the humanist, uplifting strain of "deep house" that affiliated itself with the R&B tradition, combining Philly's silky symphonic strings and mellifluous vocals with gospel's imagery of salvation: songs like Sterling Void's "It's Alright," and

Joe Smooth's "Promised Land" and album *Rejoice*. In house, there's a divide between finding yourself (through becoming a member of the house) and losing yourself (in solipsistic hallucinatory bliss). This split could be compared to the tension in gay culture between the politics of pride, unity, and collective resilience, and the more hardcore "erotic politics" of impersonal sexual encounters, "deviant" practices, and drugs.

House offered a sense of communion and community to those whose sexuality might have alienated them from organized religion. Frankie Knuckles described the Warehouse as "church for people who have fallen from grace," while another house pioneer, Marshall Jefferson, likened house to "old-time religion in the way that people just get happy and screamin'." Male divas like Daryl Pandy and Robert Owens had trained in church choirs. In "deep house" the inspirational lyrics often echo the civil rights movement of the sixties—Joe Smooth's "Promised Land" and Db's "I Have a Dream" explicitly evoke Martin Luther King—conflating the quest for black civic dignity with the struggle for gay pride. In the Children's "Freedom," a spoken-word monologue beseeches "don't oppress me" and "don't judge me," and asks, bewildered and vulnerable: "can't you accept me for what I am?" The name the Children itself comes from Chicago house slang: to be a "child" was to be gay, a member of house's surrogate family. . . .

Sonic Impact: New York's Garage Sound

By 1988 house music was having a massive impact in Britain and Europe, but Chicago itself was in decline. The previous year, the authorities had begun to crack down on the house scene, with the police banning after-hours parties and withholding late-night licenses from clubs. WBMX went off the air in 1988, and sales of house records slowed in Chicago, eventually dwindling to an average of fifteen hundred copies, a mere tenth of peak sales. Many of the scene's prime movers became inactive, disillusioned by bad deals. Others went to Europe, where financial prospects were better. Frankie Knuckles moved back to New York. DJ Pierre moved to New Jersey in 1990 and became a major exponent of house's next phase, the New York–based song-oriented deep-house sound known as "garage."

Garage's roots go back to New York's early-seventies disco underground. Mostly gay (black and Hispanic), this scene was characterized by a bacchanalian fervor fueled by acid, amphetamine, and the Ecstasy-like downer Quaalude. It was in this milieu—clubs like the Gallery, Salvation, Sanctuary, the Loft, the Ginza, and with DJs like Francis Grosso, David Rodriguez, Steve D'Aquisto, Michael Cappello, Walter Gibbons, David Mancuso—that Frankie Knuckles and his colleague Larry Levan learned the art of mixing. Garage is named in homage to the sonic sensibility and sensurround ambiance Levan developed at his legendary club, the Paradise Garage. As a distinct genre, though, it only really took shape after the club shut its doors in late 1987.

Opened in January 1977, the Paradise Garage was named after its location: an indoor truck parking lot in SoHo. Like Chicago's Warehouse, the Saturday-night clientele was gay (Friday night was mixed straight and gay). Philly and Salsoul were the soundtrack, with the songs' gospel-derived exhortations to freedom and fraternity creating a sort of pleasure-principled religious atmosphere. John Iozia described the Garage as both pagan ("an anthropologist's wet dream . . . tribal and totally anti-Western") and ecclesiastical (the dance floor was a fervent congregation of "space-age Baptists"). Just as regulars used to call the Gallery "Saturday Mass," and Salvation was styled a cathedral, Garage veterans regarded the club as "their church." The young Levan had in fact been an altar boy at an Episcopalian church, while the Bozak DJ-mixer he used at the Garage was modeled on an audio mixer originally developed for church sound systems.

Levan was one of the very first examples of the DJ-as-shaman, a technomystic who developed a science of total sound in order to create spiritual experiences for his followers. Working in tandem with engineer Richard Long, he custom-built the Garage's sound system, developing his own speakers and a special low-end-intensive subwoofer known as Larry's Horn. Later, during his all-night DJ-ing stints he would progressively upgrade the cartridges on his three turntables so that the sensory experience would peak around 5 AM. During the week, he would spend hours adjusting the positioning of speakers and making sure the sound was phys-

ically overwhelming yet crystal clear. Garage veterans testify that the sheer sonic impact of the system seemed to wreak submolecular changes in the body. . . .

"Deep"

If one word sums up the garage aesthetic, it's "deep" (hence tracks like Hardrive's "Deep Inside" and band names like Deep Dish). "Deep" captures the most progressive aspect of garage, its immersive, dub-inflected production, but also its traditionalism—a fetish for songs and classy diva vocals, an allegiance to soul and R&B, and an aura of adult-oriented maturity. Of all the post-house, post-techno styles, garage places the highest premium on conventional notions of musicality. Garage has little truck with the rhetoric of futurism; samplers and synthesizers are used for economic reasons, as a cut-rate way of emulating the opulent production values and sumptuous orchestral arrangements of classic disco like Philly and Salsoul.

After the Paradise Garage's demise in late 1987, the spirit of garage was preserved at clubs like the Sound Factory, Better Days, and Zanzibar, by DJs like Junior Vasquez, Bruce Forrest, and Tony Humphries. In the nineties, DJ/producers like Masters at Work, Roger Sanchez, David Morales, Benji Candelario, and Erick Morillo kept the flame alive. In Britain, garage thrived as a kind of back-to-basics scene for sophisticates who'd either outgrown rave or had always recoiled from its juvenile raucousness. In South London, the Ministry of Sound modeled itself on the Paradise Garage, creating an ambiance of upwardly mobile exclusivity and priding itself on having the best sound system in the world (a claim that has not gone undisputed).

The Role of Dance in the Club Experience

Kai Fikentscher

Both rave and club culture may take their cues from the DJs who get the party started, but the dancers are what transform mere gatherings into genuine cultural expressions. In this excerpt from her book, *"You Better Work!": Underground Dance Music in New York City,* ethnomusicologist Kai Fikentscher examines the communal ritual of dancing as a pleasurable sort of "work" in which the dancers and the DJ form a reciprocal circuit of social energy. Focusing primarily on the African American and gay dance club scenes in New York City, Fikentscher claims that the club environment allows for the dissolution of racial, ethnic, sexual, and gender boundaries—however fleetingly—permitting socially marginalized people a sense of belonging.

FROM THE PERSPECTIVE OF THE DJ BOOTH, THE dance floor is the central area of a dance venue. It provides the space for dancing as the main focus of the DJ. While his performance is in most cases a one-person affair, dancing almost always involves more than one person (although there may be moments when the dance floor is occupied by only one dancer or none at all). As the musical program is sent from the DJ booth through the sound system onto the dance floor, feedback flows from the floor to the DJ booth, mainly, but not exclusively,

■

Kai Fikentscher, *"You Better Work!": Underground Dance Music in New York City.* Hanover, NH: Wesleyan University Press, 2000. Copyright © 2000 by Kai Fikentscher. All rights reserved. Reproduced by permission of the publisher.

in the form of multiple bodily responses, that is, dancing. . . .

Paradise Garage, a Manhattan club that closed its doors in September 1987, was and still is regarded as having been the most influential underground dance venue in New York City. To this day many members in the underground dance scene consider it to have constituted the epitome of social dancing as a celebration of individuality and community at the same time. Dance records produced after 1987 have invoked the club's name more often than any other venue in New York by either mix or song title. Kevin Hedge, a member of Blaze, a New Jersey–based dance music production team, reminisced in an article about the Paradise Garage that reads like an obituary: ". . . in the Garage, we had blacks, Anglos, Jews, Spanish, gays, straights, everybody in one situation with a peaceful thing on their mind." Ever since its closing, promoters and hosts at other clubs (and not just in New York, but as far as London or Tokyo) have been trying to recapture the sound, image, and ambiance of the Paradise Garage, referring to their clientele as "family, we're all family in here.". . .

Inside an underground dance venue, like Paradise Garage or Sound Factory [another Manhattan club], it matters less whether the individual dancer is female or male, gay or straight, as long as the collective spirit, "the vibe in the house," is one of mutual tolerance and goodwill. Repeatedly, I have heard promoters at such venues invoke this imagery when addressing their clientele over a microphone. In these clubs where the majority of patrons are often male or African American or both, dancers dance alone or with dancers of the same or the opposite sex, doing perhaps one of several versions of the hustle. Nondancing men and women who may form a circle of spectators around one, two, or three dancers dancing hip-hop, freestyle, or vogue. More typically, the dance movements are at the individual dancer's discretion and not prescribed (except for the occasional group routine or line dance where half the floor may spontaneously join to step in formation, doing the Bus Stop or the Electric Slide). One may dance alone, anonymously, or interact with other dancers, by making eye contact, exchanging verbal comments, or copying a certain step, and taking turns with him or her in front of a crowd of spectators. Playful competition is often central in a group of male peers who

take turns trying to "burn" each other with very original combinations or technically or athletically demanding moves, while the competitors look on and may give intermittent applause and/or shouts of encouragement or compliments. Dancing (also deejaying) is frequently referred to as "Working (it) out," as "Work it!" or as "You better work!"—the corresponding encouragement or compliment to a particular dancer's (or DJ's) performance. This use of "work"—which might be seen as an African American inversion of the central concept of the Anglo-American Protestant work ethic—is also reflected in the titles of many records.

Archie Burnett, who has danced in New York underground clubs on a regular basis since 1981, considers his dancing a physical and mental workout. In his words, the DJ's efforts behind the turntables translate directly into the dancer's domain: "As you walk in, you hear and smell the sounds, which get your blood pumping and adrenaline flowing. The club itself is a mood changer. You may have had the worst day, but when you are in there for two hours, your mood will change. It's about music, energy, spirituality, all in one. But you must give yourself over to it. You have no choice because the DJ is going to make you work." This type of effect on the body by the music is described in similar terms by [author of *Night Dancin'* Vita] Miezitis: "As you approach, even from a distance, you can already hear the faint beat, feel it reverberating ever so slightly in the pavement. It pulses like a heartbeat, growing with every step toward the disco entrance. . . . As you enter, electricity shoots through the air in all directions. The energy flows from the music and the lights and the crowd, from inside yourself. . . . Throughout the night, as more and more people come to a disco, the energy level builds and the interaction between the deejay and crowd intensifies."

Showcase Performances

Besides the performance by a DJ and those of his dancers, there is yet another type of performance to be found inside a dance venue: that of the "showcase" disco artist or singer. A showcase takes place on a performance stage during a specific time (usually an hour or two after midnight) set aside by the venue's management or the promoter, and is usually a combi-

nation of live vocals and a playback tape. Often, the purpose of showcases is to promote a recently issued record of the performer in question (usually a single vocalist). In club terminology, the supreme compliment is to bestow on such a performer the title "diva," a compliment always given by men, most of them gay, many of them African American, to a female who is most often African American as well. Vocalists such as Donna Summer, Gloria Gaynor, Grace Jones, Rochelle Fleming, Loleatta Holloway, Martha Wash, Kim Mazelle, or Adeva are loved and adored as "divas" by their mostly male and largely gay fans. Club appearances by these "stars" of club music are best witnessed on so-called gay nights, when predominantly, but not exclusively gay audiences are known to respond to the performances of their idols more enthusiastically than straight crowds do on "straight" nights. Often during these performances, a bond between performer and audience is celebrated: both the divas, as African-American females, and their audiences, whether Caucasian, Latino, or African-American gay men, are in more than one way "others" in a society based on Western Judeo-Christian values and standards that have historically reinforced the marginalization of its minorities of Latinos, African-Americans, gays and lesbians. Nonetheless, some consider the popular image of the black diva problematic, as it may signify a gendered form of racism among white gay men, which in turn bespeaks the status of women in mainstream American society in general.

If matters of privacy, etiquette, self-presentation, and sexual expression are able to be redefined via club dancing, the dance itself then is an act that has the potential to liberate the self (mind/body) from dominant modes of thinking and behavior. Dancing thus can have an educational function, impacting the way one thinks about oneself as a gendered human being, and/or about others who may belong to a different ethnic group, and/or may express a different sexual orientation. Dancing may reflect or amplify the social conditioning of one's gender, just as it may enhance the concept of one's own gender and sexuality. It can also question or even subvert these constructs ever so playfully. This option of playful subversion can facilitate the issue of self-expression in public, which is particularly relevant to those whose expressions place them at

the margins of American society. . . .

Types of gender construction and of expressions of sexuality that do not necessarily conform with mainstream values are characteristic of underground dance culture. Dancing, then, is not merely one form of musical consumption. As long as the dancer is on the floor, he or she is performing, either for him- or herself, for one or several dance partners, or for the DJ. Collectively, all dancers, through the sum total of many individual performances, offer the DJ a performance encompassing the entire dance floor. The feedback of this collective performance is the crucial instrument by which the DJ can evaluate the appeal of his program. By monitoring the dance floor, a good DJ can gauge the type of music his audience likes to dance to most—although this is hardly a constant, as the population on the floor is in constant flux as the night goes on. . . .

So far, I have discussed deejaying and dancing as autonomous, yet interdependent expressive activities, and as such, characteristic traits of UDM [underground dance music] in New York. Accordingly, spinning is the DJ's domain, and involves the creative use of his equipment—records, turntables, mixer, and a sound system. Working it out is determined by each individual dancer's efforts. He or she determines the degree to which the dance will interact not only with the music, but also with the dancing of others on the same floor. While the variables of space, lighting, musical program, and other factors contributing to the "vibe" may be reflected, the dance itself is an autonomous individual creation (freestyle) and its author is at liberty to determine the degree to which elements of certain dance styles (for example, hustle, vogue, breakdancing) may be incorporated. Yet spinning and dancing are closely interdependent. A good DJ will animate his dancers to react to his music; in turn, ferocious and/or creative dancing will prompt a DJ to program and mix his music correspondingly. . . .

The concept of collective performance is central to a discussion of underground dancing. While the idea of performance applies equally to the DJ and the dancer, it is the multiplication, across a densely populated dance floor, of each individual dancer's physical response that gives club dancing its collective character as it transforms sound into movement in a generally unstructured and playful fashion.

Club Cultures and Neo-Tribes

Andy Bennett

Andy Bennett, lecturer in sociology at the University
of Surrey in England, brings the methods of sociological analysis to bear on what has come to be known as
"club culture." According to Bennett, club culture is
not a single, uniform culture, but rather a plurality of
distinct alternative communities spread across the
globe. These communities, or "neo-tribes," share certain common features, such as a desire for "'togetherness' based on . . . fun, relaxation and pleasure." However, Bennett finds that club cultures are resilient and
adaptable, often addressing the specific needs of clubbers who wish to set themselves apart from their particular mainstream cultural frameworks.

THE MEANING AND SIGNIFICANCE OF 'DANCE
music' has altered substantially since the 1970s when the term
was synonymous with discotheque or 'disco'. Disco was generally considered to be the antithesis of more 'serious' 1970s
musics such as hard rock, 'progressive' rock and, latterly, punk.
Fans of these genres were often heard to mock what they considered to be the centrally defining characteristics of disco: ef-
fete melodies, trite lyrics and a commercially driven production ethic. With notable exceptions, such as [cultural critic
Richard] Dyer (1979) whose work focuses on the significance
of disco for gay culture, disco and other forms of dance music
were also denied serious academic attention during the 1970s
and the early part of the 1980s. This scenario is in extreme

■

Andy Bennett, *Cultures of Popular Music*. Buckingham, UK: Open University Press,
2001. Copyright © 2001 by Andy Bennett. All rights reserved. Reproduced by permission of the Open University Press/McGraw-Hill Publishing Company.

contrast to the 1990s, which saw the transformation of dance music into a highly 'serious', often critically acclaimed and academically scrutinized genre. Certainly, contemporary dance music often becomes commercial chart music, much as dance music in the 1970s did. However, a comparison of contemporary dance music acts, such as the Prodigy and the Aphex Twin, with 1970s dance music artists, for example ABBA and the Bee Gees, begins to illustrate how both the fan base for dance music and the sensibilities of the artists themselves have changed. . . .

A New Moral Panic

A similar public reaction [to that which greeted punk rock in the late 1970s] was prompted by the media with the arrival of house in British clubs during the late 1980s where it quickly acquired the tag 'acid house' due to its associations with a newly available amphetamine based stimulant known as Ecstasy or 'E'. In many ways acid house presented far more opportunities for the media to expose a potential threat to young people than punk had done. Punk, for all the dangers that the media linked with it, had at least been a highly visual form of youth culture, a 'spectacular' form of shock tactic which relied upon public exposure to achieve its desired effect. Acid house, however, was an altogether different phenomenon. Rather than relying on a stylistic 'intrusion' of public space, acid house made use of abandoned inner-city spaces such as disused warehouses and factories. [University of York professor Antonio] Melechi suggests that such a retreat from public space was linked to acid house's emphasis upon the 'ecstasy of disappearance':

> While subcultural refusals have been traditionally effected through the statement of self-expression and the display of alternative identity, Acid house has relinquished this ground. . . . The strategy of resistance to the scene of identity necessitates an escape from the (media) gaze, as, unlike previous subcultures which remain 'hiding in the light', a whole subculture attempts to vanish.

The result of acid house's attempts to evade the media gaze was a moral crusade on the part of the tabloid press.

Labelled a 'Killer Cult', acid house was portrayed by the

media as something intrinsically evil that would brainwash young people and lure them away from the safety of the family home to a dark and secretive world of drug taking and immoral behaviour. The fact that acid house was the first youth movement since the 1960s to refer openly to drug use further enhanced the media's ability to portray it in a wholly sinister fashion. Indeed, 'acid house' is itself a media created term inspired by the alleged parallels between house and 1960s psychedelia. The uncanny resonance suggested by the media between acid house and psychedelia was further enhanced by the fact that these two movements occurred exactly 20 years apart. The summer of 1987, it was proclaimed, was the 'Second Summer of Love'. Significantly, however, the tabloid press was not the only voice heard in the debate regarding acid house. [Cultural historian Sarah] Thornton suggests that one of the things which set the house scene apart from previous chapters in youth cultural history was the presence of a 'niche' media, that is, magazines, fanzines and so on catering specifically for young clubbers, which scrutinized the reporting of the mainstream media and offered alternative accounts. Such a reaction on the part of the 'niche' media was seen in the wake of the sensationalized mainstream media reports which compared acid house with psychedelia. Thus, for example, *Face* journalist Peter Nasmyth wrote of the drug Ecstasy:

> It can make you feel very close and empathetic—you might feel like hugging your friends—but the affection it inspires is unlikely to send anyone into the frenzied raptures common in the Haight/Ashbury district in 1967. Ecstasy is a misleading name; the drug is so called more for reasons of promotion than resolution.

Despite such alternative reporting of acid house and its attendant drug culture, however, it was the sensationalism of the tabloid press headlines which gripped the public's imagination during the late 1980s. As a direct consequence of the media attention centred upon it, acid house became a focus of deep concern for the parent culture and other moral guardians. Indeed, reactions to acid house were not limited to public outcry but also involved large-scale state intervention. Nightclubs which featured rave events were subject to random spot checks by the

police and in some cases had their licences revoked. Similarly, in 1991, former Conservative MP [Member of Parliament] for Luton South Graham Bright's Entertainments (Increased Penalties) Act outlawed the staging of large scale unlicensed raves and warehouse parties. Further restrictions were placed upon the rave scene with the implementation of the Criminal Justice and Public Order Act 1994, particularly section 63 of the Act which gives the police authority 'to remove persons attending or preparing for a rave'. According to the Act, a rave may be classed as any 'gathering on land in the open air of 100 or more persons (whether or not trespassers) at which amplified music is played during the night'. The Act further states that '"land in the open air" includes a place partly open to the air' while '"music" includes sounds wholly or predominantly characterized by the emission of a succession of repetitive beats'.

'Club Cultures' and 'Neo-Tribes'

Despite such authoritative reactions and the legal sanctions placed upon events featuring house and techno, dance music gained in popularity. Indeed, subsequent years saw house and techno diversify into an increasingly complex range of subgenres. Similarly, new forms of dance music, notably 'jungle' emerged. The club-based dance music scene of the 1990s gave rise to a new sociological term 'club cultures'. . . .

In [1993], journalist Tim Willis wrote an article for the *Sunday Times* entitled 'The lost tribes' in which he [observed]:

> Young men with shaved heads and pigtails, stripped to the waist, are executing vaguely oriental hand movements. Freeze-framed by strobes in clouds of dry ice, revivalist hippies and mods are swaying in the maelstrom. Rastas, ragga girls, ravers there is no stylistic cohesion to the assembly, as there would have been in the (g)olden days of youth culture.

In truth, this extreme merging of visual styles was a short-lived spectacle. It is clear that the visual image of youth is becoming increasingly a matter of individual choice as young people construct and reconstruct their image and identity with reference to what [cultural anthropologist Ted] Polhemus terms 'a supermarket of style'. At the same time, however, the splitting and resplitting of dance music genres has ensured that those

who once mixed in the common space of the dance floor are now able to find musics and clubs that cater more specifically for particular 'types' of clubber. . . .

In my own research on dance music I examine the issue of temporality and club culture using [sociology professor Michel] Maffesoli's concept of *tribus* or neo-tribes. Underpinning Maffesoli's concept of tribes is a concern to illustrate the increasingly fluid and unstable nature of social relations in contemporary society. According to Maffesoli, the tribe is 'without the rigidity of the forms of organization with which we are familiar, it refers more to a certain ambience, a state of mind, and is preferably to be expressed through lifestyles that favour appearance and form. . . .

Drawing upon such theoretical observations in my own work I argue that the dance club setting provides a vivid example of the tribal associations that Maffesoli [and others] suggest characterize contemporary society. Providing a space for expressions of 'togetherness' based on articulations of fun, relaxation and pleasure, the club setting can be seen as one of many forms of temporal engagement through which such neo-tribal associations are formed. Indeed, in many of the larger clubs which feature urban dance music nights, the desire of the clubber to choose from and engage with a variety of different crowds has been further enhanced through the use of different rooms or floors as a means of staging parallel dance events with club-goers free to move between these events as they please. Consequently, the clubbing experience is becoming increasingly a matter of individual choice, the type of music heard and the setting in which it is heard and danced to being very much the decision of the individual consumer. Significantly, such factors in turn have a marked influence on the way in which clubbers talk about the actual process of music consumption. Thus, for many clubbers, 'clubbing' appears to be regarded less as a singularly definable activity and more as a series of fragmented, temporal experiences as they move between different dance floors and engage with different crowds.

This is clearly illustrated in the following discussion extract in which I asked a group of regular attenders of a particular club event in Newcastle to describe the nature of the event to me:

A.B.:   How would you describe 'Pigbag'? What kind of an event is it?

Diane: Well, I would say um, it's a different experience depending upon . . .

Shelly: Upon what's on . . .

Diane: What music's on and what floor you're on as well.

A.B.:   I know there are different things going on on each floor.

All: Yeah.

Rob: There's three types of thing going on actually. There's like the sort of cafe room which plays hip hop and jazz and then downstairs there's more singing sort of house music . . . and upstairs there's eh . . . well how could you describe that?

Debbie: Well it's quite sort of eh . . . the more housey end of techno music with sort of like trancey techno . . . the sort of easier, comfortable side of techno.

Diane: Yeah and then you'll get people moving between all three floors and checking out what's going on. . . .

Dance Music and New Social Movements

Despite the case which can be made for the inherently unstable and fleeting nature of the collective associations between dance club audiences, contemporary dance music, by nature of its attraction for disempowered and disaffected young people, has also played a significant role in inspiring a series of proactive socio-political movements, including Reclaim the Streets and the Anti-Road Protest. Collectively referred to as the DiY [Do it Yourself] protest movement, such activities have, according to [RtS activist John] Jordan, broken 'down the barriers between art and protest [using] new forms of creative and poetic resistance'. Jordan examines how 'new creative political methods, using direct action, performance art, sculpture and installation' have been used to mount strategies of resistance to environmental threats from new road-building schemes and mounting air pollution caused through the congestion of city streets. According to Jordan, the effectiveness of this form of resistance results from the spectacle that it creates, 'not only [for] the media, but for local passersby, who are often awestruck by what they see and are thus brought into dialogue about the issues'.

Raves and other dance music festivals have also given rise to alternative lifestyles built around self-sufficient communities that closely approximate the commune experiments of the late 1960s. A pertinent example of this is the Exodus Collective. Originally part of the British dance party scene, which organized free raves around Britain during the late 1980s, Exodus occupied disused farm buildings near the town of Luton, in Bedfordshire, and transformed them into a housing cooperative which became known as HAZ (Housing Action Zone). Initially threatened with expulsion by the Department of Transport, which owned the buildings, Exodus was subsequently granted tenancy of the farm after department representatives visited the site and noted the scale and quality of restoration work carried out by Exodus members on the occupied buildings. As [journalist Tim] Malyon observes:

> extensive renovation was carried out on the farm buildings, as well as a bungalow and house where collective members now live. Almost all the wood was recycled from pallets donated by local businesses. There's a growing herd of animals, including horses, goats, a bullock, sheep, ducks and several love-struck Vietnamese pot-bellied pigs. The plan is to open the farm up to the public, and especially local schools. . . .

In so far as dance music culture can be seen in part as a reaction to the economic and social austerity of contemporary Britain, it is not simply encouraging the discourse of retreatism suggested, for example, in Melechi's notion of an 'ecstasy of disappearance'. On the contrary, dance music culture can also be seen to be encouraging attitudes among the young which are proactive. The Exodus Collective is illustrative of how dance music's capacity for bringing people together in the common space of the rave has functioned to produce a more concrete series of lifestyle strategies through which individuals engage with the social circumstances that confront them.

Rave New World

Christopher John Farley

What is it that makes devotees out of those who have experienced the energy of the dance floor? Christopher John Farley, a renowned music critic, novelist (*My Favorite War*), and senior writer for *Time* magazine, analyzes the combination of throbbing beats, pulsing lights, intoxicants, and giddy liberation that attract young people to legitimate clubs and illegal raves alike. In order to explain the various thrills and pleasures of what can be termed (however loosely) the rave "movement," Farley compares raves to the Beat movement that defined the alternative youth culture of the 1950s and early 1960s. By drawing this analogy, Farley argues that raves deserve to be regarded as legitimate forms of artistic and social expression.

IT'S HARD TO TALK TO WOMEN AT RAVES, SAYS Ben Wilke. The big beats drown out small talk. If you really need to, you can go to a "chill-out" room for get-to-know-you conversation. And if you really need them, there's "a moderate amount of drugs," says the 17-year-old from Houston. But for him, raves are "all about the music." Says Wilke: "Real party kids don't do drugs. We go to dance and have a good time." He goes on: "A lot of people don't understand it, but the guitar thing's been done. Electronic music is all I listen to. It beats my heart."

First we had the Beat Generation; now we have the Beats-per-Minute Generation. And it's not just about ecstasy.

Simply defined, a rave is a party—often an all-night-long party—at which some form of electronic, or "techno," music is played, usually by a deejay. A rave can be as small as 25 people

■

Christopher John Farley, "Rave New World," *Time*, June 5, 2000. Copyright © 2000 by Time, Inc. All rights reserved. Reproduced by permission.

or larger than 25,000. And while raves have been around [since the early 1990s], the rituals, visuals and sounds associated with raves have finally started to exert a potent influence on pop music, advertising and even computer games. Several new films about raves are either in theaters or coming soon, including the British comedy *Human Traffic* and the documentaries *Better Living Through Circuitry* and *Rise*, a study of the rave scene in New Orleans. Says Jason Jordan, co-author of *Searching for the Perfect Beat*, a new book about raves and visual art: "Rave culture is youth culture right now."

"Rave culture is affecting pop culture in ways similar to the Beat Generation—and it's being misinterpreted in the same way," says Greg Harrison, director of the [2000] movie *Groove*, a fictional take on the rave scene. "In the case of the Beats, a complex and subtle ethos was distilled by pop culture to marijuana, goatees and poetry. I would argue that just as there was much more to the Beats, there's something more subtle and interesting about the rave scene."

To find a rave, you can pick up one of the artfully rendered flyers at cafes or cool record stores like Other Music in New York City or Atomic Music in Houston. Or you might surf the Net and check out sites like ravedata.com or rave.com. Or you might just ask a friend in the know. Raves have traditionally been held in venues without permits or permission, giving them an outlaw allure. Today, however, an increasing number of raves are legal ones, and places like [the now defunct] Twilo in New York City specialize in re-creating the rave feel in legitimate clubs. "The New York club scene was not about music until Twilo opened," says Paul van Dyk, a popular deejay who specializes in trance—a soft, transporting form of techno and one of the genre's many, many offshoots.

Ravers often wear loose, wide-legged jeans that flare out at the bottom. Knickknacks from childhood, like suckers, pacifiers and dolls, are common accessories. Dancers, sweating to the music all night, often carry bottles of water to battle dehydration, which can be aggravated by ecstasy. Attendees sometimes dress in layers so clothes can be stripped off if the going gets hot, and blue and green flexible glow sticks are popular. One sound you'll hear if the party's going right: a communal whoop of approval when the deejay starts riding a good groove.

"The first rock-'n'-roll shows were dance events," says 6th Element promoter Matt E. Silver, who has worked with best-selling electronica acts such as Chemical Brothers and Prodigy. "Now it's about deejay culture." In the movie *Groove*, the filmmakers refer to that connection between deejay and dancer, between promoter and satisfied raver, as "the nod." Many rave promoters and deejays don't do it for the money. They do it for the nod.

One electronic musician who is definitely getting the nod these days is the American deejay-composer Moby. Most deejays a decade ago were faceless shadows lurking behind turntables. Now deejays associated with the rave scene—like Van Dyk, Armand Van Helden, Keoki and BT—are artists, celebrities, superstars. "If [twentieth-century modernist composer, Igor] Stravinsky were alive today, this is the kind of music he'd make," says BT, who composed music for the rave movie *Go* (1999) as well as the PlayStation game *Die Hard Trilogy*. "It just affords you a broader sonic palette to work from."

Moby has used his palette skillfully. He got his start as a deejay, but he also sings and plays with a backing band when he's on tour. His 1995 album *Everything Is Wrong* sold about 125,000 copies. His critically acclaimed [1999] album *Play*, which samples old blues songs and sets them to futuristic beats has already gone platinum. The rave scene is catching on with a new generation of fans, Moby believes, because it offers an alternative to today's version of bubblegum. "The consolidation of all the different record companies under big multinational parent companies," he says, has spawned the current crush of mass-produced teen pop acts. "Your BMGs, your Sonys, your Time Warners . . . nothing against these companies, but they buy music companies and they expect music to perform the way that, say, snack cakes or liquid paper performs. There's so much commercial emphasis on disposable pop music that I think it leaves a lot of people desperately looking for other types of musical expression."

One of the most creative ways in which rave culture expresses itself is its party flyers. These handouts are to raves what graffiti art is to hip-hop and psychedelic posters were to the acid rock of the '70s. They give vision to rave's sounds. Sometimes—much like rappers' sampling old songs—they ap-

propriate corporate logos with ironic visual twists. The MasterCard logo becomes "MasterRave," or Rice Krispies becomes "Rave Krisp E's." Other flyers employ 3-D images and wild metallic hues that draw inspiration from sci-fi films, anime, even the rounded, flower-power imagery of the Summer of Love. "In a lot of ways it's one of the most modern visual art forms you can see," says Eric Paxton Stauder, a member of Dots per Minute, a network of designers that focuses on rave flyers. "Stylistically, you see things in flyers that you don't see other places—uses of line work and fontography. It's open and unrestricted, and it's a testing ground for combining visual elements together."

Rave iconography is already being co-opted by Madison Avenue, which has learned all about digging up the underground and selling the dirt. TV ads for Toyota's Echo have the trippy look and feel of rave flyers (Toyota is sponsoring a U.S. tour of British electronica acts Groove Armada and Faze Action). Every song on Moby's 18-track album *Play* has been licensed, popping up in ads for the last episode of *Party of Five*, movies like *The Beach* and commercials for Nissan's Altima sedan and Quest minivan. Donna Karan's DKNY label plans to use deejay John Digweed's song "Heaven Scent" to promote a fragrance with the same name.

Wayne Friedman, entertainment-marketing reporter for *Advertising Age*, says today's admakers look to tap into underground movements quickly so that they can make use of sounds and images that aren't necessarily familiar but that pique interest. Acts like Moby fit the bill. Says Friedman: "It's almost like you can't be overly commercial when you're trying to make commercials."

Many ravers are wary and weary of the media's embrace. In particular, many believe that the press is more interested in writing about drugs than about the music—and that the press coverage is partly to blame for the supposed ecstasy boom. Says Jon Reiss, director of *Better Living Through Circuitry*: "The media hype says if you want to do drugs, come to these parties. So all these kids come to the parties looking for drugs. It becomes a self-fulfilling prophecy."

Indeed, some of the biggest acts associated with the rave scene say they are drug free. Van Dyk says he was introduced

to electronic music in East Germany, when he secretly tuned in to West German radio as a kid. He didn't need drugs to enjoy the music then, so he figures he doesn't need them now. Moby says he tried smoking pot when he was 11 or 12 so he could hang out with the "cool kids," but that was pretty much the end of his experimentation. Says Moby: "I've never tried ecstasy, I've never tried cocaine, I've never tried heroin. I don't think there's anything ethically wrong with drug use, but the reason I stay away from it is that I value my brain too much. I don't want to trust my synapses to some stranger that I met in a nightclub. I hope to use my brain for the rest of my life."

We hope he does too. Every few years somebody says electronic music is going to break out, that electronic acts are going to storm the charts. A couple of years ago, Prodigy and the Chemical Brothers were supposed to lead the charge. They sold well, but few like-minded acts shared their success. This year [in 2000] it's Moby, and perhaps acts like Alice Deejay and others will follow. Maybe this time rave culture is here to stay . . . or maybe it'll slip safely back into the underground with alternative rock. With horrifyingly generic teen-pop acts blaring out from MTV's *Total Request Live* day in and day out, it's a wonder more kids haven't turned to drugs to escape the awful racket. Sure, a fair amount of electronica is wordless wallpaper, but slip on Moby's soulful, cerebral *Play*, and you won't need any substances to get high. The music will take you there all by itself.

Techno in the Mainstream and on TV

Michael Paoletta

Michael Paoletta's assessment of the commercialization of the dance and rave scenes offers an argument against those who decry the use of electronic music in advertising as the death of the "pure" rave experience. Paoletta, a contributing writer for *Billboard* magazine, argues that electronica has proven to be an ideal sound track for television commercials and programs that wish to target the coveted eighteen- to thirty-four-year-old consumer base. By the same token, notes Paoletta, exposure on television has provided record labels with a new and highly successful way to promote dance and electronica artists to a much wider audience than previously possible. Paoletta goes so far as to applaud artists such as Moby, Crystal Method, Dirty Vegas, and others for having the foresight to benefit from an inevitable trend.

IN THE PAST, ARTISTS WERE RELUCTANT TO LIcense their music for use in TV commercials. But artists like Moby and Dido changed the rules when they successfully licensed their music for third-party use in a variety of mediums, including, respectively, the small-screen world of TV commercials and popular weekly series. In the years since, placing music in TV commercials and TV shows has become a viable,

■

Michael Paoletta, "Seen as the Perfect Mix of Commerce and Art, Millions of Consumers Are Being Turned On to Dance and Electronic Music Through Their Televisions," *Billboard*, March 22, 2003, p. 39. Copyright © 2003 by VNU Business Media. Reproduced by permission.

as well as increasingly competitive, way to break, market and promote dance/electronic artists, particularly when there are less adventurous souls at radio and video networks willing to take a chance with the genre.

"Radio is incredibly genre-specific and pigeonholed in its programming," says Neil Gillis, VP of A&R and advertising at Warner-Chappell Music. "That appears to limit radio's listening audience, down to the proposed demographic of that programming model. Conversely, companies that smartly and creatively utilize music think they can reach a wider audience by a great use of any kind of music, as long as it serves the ultimate message well."

For recent proof, look no further than British trio Dirty Vegas' "Days Go By." [In spring 2002] the song became the soundtrack to the Mitsubishi Eclipse TV-ad campaign. While the act's U.S. label, Capitol, had planned on doing a major club campaign first, it had to immediately shift gears. The popularity of the TV commercial—with the pop-locking girl—created demand at radio and on dancefloors for the infectious track. Thanks to Mitsubishi, the track took on a life of its own. To date, the eponymous album from which "Days Go By" is culled has scanned more than 500,000 units, according to SoundScan.

"The ad helped push our record into everybody's living room," says Dirty Vegas member Paul Harris. "Only now is radio in America starting to play more dance music. So, people seeing the ad on TV, and hearing our music, contacted their local radio stations wanting to hear the song. The power of the people is what helped propel our song to success."

Ditto for French trio Télépopmusik's "Breathe." When originally released [in 2002], the dreamy Catalogue/Capitol single was only embraced by a handful of trend-setting radio DJs, including KCRW Santa Monica's Nic Harcourt and Jason Bentley. [In late 2002] the song was introduced to the U.S. mainstream via its inclusion in the Mitsubishi Outlander TV ad. As a result of that exposure, U.S. sales of the act's album, *Genetic World*, are approaching 70,000 units.

"Mitsubishi wanted a track that was new and current," says Ron Broitman, VP of film/TV music at BMG Music Publishing, which oversees Télépopmusik's repertoire. "This gives the brand credibility with its targeted younger demographic. In the

end, the combination of visuals and music becomes larger than the individual parts."

A Marriage of Commerce and Art

Vincent Picardi, senior VP/associate creative director of advertising agency Deutsch, responsible for Mitsubishi's successful and popular "Are You In?" campaign, concurs. "We see it as the perfect marriage of commerce and art," he explains. "Music spurs sales of Mitsubishi cars and vice versa. Mitsubishi understands the eclectic nature of music and how it works with their brand. Artists and labels see what this exposure does for them." Indeed.

Neither major nor independent acts are afraid to mix commerce and art. In recent months, TV commercials have introduced mainstream America to a wealth of groovy sounds, encompassing Fatboy Slim's "Because We Can" (Coors Light), Timo Maas' "To Get Down" (Dodge), Lemon Jelly's "The Staunton Lick" (Volkswagen), Basement Jaxx's "Where's Your Head At?" (Intel), the Chemical Brothers' "Galaxy Bounce" (Sirius), Groove Armada's "Groove Is In" (Sprite), BT's "The Revolution" (Mitsubishi), Crystal Method's "Busy Child" (the Gap), Jay-Jay Johanson's "Automatic Lover" (2[x]ist) and Gotan Project's "Santa Maria" (Skyy Vodka), among others.

"One year ago [in 2002], and even with Moby's success, none of my co-workers were focusing on this area," says VP head of special projects David Steel, who was a major force in licensing every track from Moby's *Play* album. "But this has drastically changed internally. Now I'm being asked why Underworld's music or Puretone's 'Addicted to Bass' are not being used in commercials. It's been a complete 180.". . .

"Over the years, people have been continuously saying that dance music will explode," notes DanceStar USA [the American Dance Music Awards] founder/CEO Andy Ruffell. "We think it will simply continue to grow each year. Now we have lots of corporate companies recognizing and understanding the dance/electronic culture and lifestyle. Marketers are realizing the genre's potential—how it reaches today's youth by being both new and exciting."

Due to the medium's millions of viewers, TV commercials and shows act as catalysts, or tipping points, notes Jonathan

McHugh, VP of creative development at Jive Records, who has licensed several Groove Armada tracks for TV use. "TV creates multiple impressions," he says. "There really is no greater tool to spread the word. This is incredibly important for dance and electronic music, which is not considered mainstream fare and which relies on clubs and specialty radio for play. But put the music in a TV commercial or show and you reach millions

Moby Assesses the State of Rave

Internationally celebrated DJ and electronic musician Moby discusses the state of rave culture with Jim DeRogatis, a pop music critic and cohost of "Sound Opinions" on WXRT-FM (93.1) in Chicago.

DeRogatis: Is there a "real" rave culture anymore?

Moby: Yes and no. My cousin, who's 16 years old, goes out to parties all the time and listens to the music and has his own fashion style, and he gets made fun of in school because of it. To me the litmus test of a subculture is if you get made fun of in school.

DeRogatis: I remember an early interview you did with the Chicago rave zine *Reactor.* At that point you were talking about how the rave community should not remain incestuous and cliquish. But it seems as if it's gone to the opposite extreme, with Fatboy Slim popping up in every other TV commercial, and the Chemical Brothers acting like [heavy metal band] Poison in front of 4,500 kids at [Chicago concert venue] the Aragon.

Moby: The good thing about mass exposure to alternative culture is that it then exposes kids who can really benefit from it, like kids in Ohio or Missouri who might otherwise have a much more blinkered, cloistered existence. The downside is that alternative cultures can then get watered down.

Jim DeRogatis, "Moby Raves On; Rocker Dodges Mainstream," *Chicago Sun-Times*, August 22, 1999, p. 11.

of people. Radio execs always ask themselves the same thing: 'Why should I play this record?' Well, if people respond to its TV placement, the question is answered."

This is precisely what happened with Dido's "Here With Me," when it became the theme song for the TV series *Roswell*. "You can't deny the fact that *Roswell* broke Dido," notes Patrick Pocklington, who oversees Nettwerk Management's DJ management group and contributes to Dido's management team. "We had a handful of radio stations on this song at the beginning. But then *Roswell* picked it up. By the show's season finale, more and more radio stations began playing the song. People were able to connect the dots between the song they had been hearing on the radio, the song they'd been hearing on *Roswell* and the artist herself."

Fans of hit cable series like HBO's *Sex and the City* and Showtime's *Queer as Folk* are regularly introduced to dance/electronic music, while a recent episode of NBC's successful *Will & Grace* spotlighted the sounds of Thunderpuss & Barnes' chart-topping club hit "Head."

A New Way to Market Music

"Part of what I've always wanted to do is promote new music and talent—especially that which might not get radio airplay," says *Queer as Folk* music supervisor Michael Perlmutter of Toronto-based S.L. Feldman & Associates. "We have 2-to-3 million viewers each week, many of whom e-mail us inquiring about the music."

For the past two [2001–2002] seasons, music featured on the show has been posted on Showtime's official Web site (queer.sho.com). "We're like a college radio station," Perlmutter adds. "We can be musically eclectic." Consider the following *Queer as Folk* selections: Darude's "Sandstorm," Madonna's "Don't Tell Me," Blur's "Song No. 2," Pet Shop Boys' "Break for Love," Crystal Method's "Wild, Sweet 'N Cool," Kosheen's "Hide U," Basement Jaxx's "Get Me Off," Björk's "Human Behaviour," Morel's "Cabaret," Kim English's "Everyday" and Daft Punk's "Harder, Better, Faster, Stronger." Last year [2002], RCA issued the *Queer as Folk: The Second Season* soundtrack, which followed the first season's 2001 collection.

Simply put, "You want your record to be heard in whatever

manner," says Scott Kirkland, one-half of Crystal Method, whose music has been featured in ads for Mazda, Mitsubishi and the Gap—and whose "Keep Hope Alive" became the opening theme for the TV show *3rd Watch*. Kirkland acknowledges that the duo's "Busy Child" became a mainstay at alternative-rock radio only after appearing in a Gap commercial.

"Music can serve many purposes," producer BT explains. "I grew up around classical snobbery. That whole way of thinking is counterproductive to artistry and creativity. TV has created an exciting way for music to be heard. It's a way for contemporary artists to stay afloat. In the end, a new model for promoting and marketing music is replacing the antiquated model that record companies are still trying to use."

It's ironic, notes New York–based music consultant John Trepp, that "For years, labels have been saying there is no way to promote dance/electronic artists. Yet you turn on the TV, and that's all you hear. So, once again, we have labels being re-actionary—it's like an accidental opportunity. In the future, perhaps labels will become more proactive, hiring an agency like Deutsch at the get-go to assist in the setup and marketing of a new act."

Or, perhaps, a company like Mitsubishi will develop its own label imprint. Adds Trepp, "Except for Mitsubishi, I can't think of one brand that has consistently stayed with an aesthetic. Mitsubishi could very well become a brand for a very stylish kind of music. The audience is already there."

EXAMINING POP CULTURE

Dancing into the New Millennium

Rave Culture: Living Dream or Living Death?

Simon Reynolds

In this selection *Spin* magazine senior editor Simon Reynolds draws on both his personal experience and professional expertise to ponder the future of rave and to examine the changes taking place in what he has termed "generation ecstasy." Looking back on the mutations of dance culture across the 1990s, Reynolds charts the erosion of rave's initial utopian idealism and the transformation of the ethos of blissful abandonment, togetherness, and euphoria into a more individualized, edgy form of disunity. Reynolds makes careful links between these changing attitudes and more recent developments in dance music—specifically drum and bass, progressive house, and garage—and concludes that the music and the culture that surrounds it are increasingly directionless and void of meaning. According to the author these changes in rave culture have resulted in part from the effects of long-term use of ecstacy as well as an increase in the use of marijuana and cocaine among rave enthusiasts.

'RAVE IS DEAD', OR SO THE PUNDITS SAY. YET there's a sense in which it's bigger than ever. Not only is the spectrum of nineties youth culture dominated by the ever-widening delta of post-rave scenes—trance, ambient, handbag house, garage, jungle, happy hardcore, gabba, Scottish bouncy

■

Simon Reynolds, "Rave Culture: Living Dream or Living Death?" *The Clubcultures Reader: Readings in Popular Cultural Studies*, edited by Steve Redhead, with Derek Wynn and Justin O'Connor. Oxford, UK: Blackwell Publishers, 1997. Copyright © 1997 by Blackwell Publishers, Ltd. All rights reserved. Reproduced by permission.

techno, Megadog-style crusty-rave, *ad infinitum*—but it also seems obvious that more people are involved in the weekender/ecstasy lifestyle than ever, as veteran ravers hang on in there, while each year produces a wave of new recruits. But as for the rave myth, the ideal of love, peace, unity, positivity—well, that's been smelling funny for quite a while.

Alive, but dead; more popular than ever, but a cultural cul-de-sac—this is, of course, how people have felt about rock music for decades. When [Sex Pistols frontman] Johnny Rotten sneered 'Ever felt like you've been cheated?' on stage at Winterlands in 1978, it was meant to be the death-knell of rock 'n' roll. Thirteen years later, with 'Smells like teen spirit', Nirvana could still find exhilarating musical life in the reiteration of Rotten's message (rebellion is a con, a sales pitch, mere grease for the wheels of commerce). Talk of the death of rock or the death of rave refers not [to] the exhaustion of the music's formal possibilities, then, but to the seeping away of meaning, the loss of a collective sense of going somewhere. This [article] looks at the ways in which rave culture—in so far as it has proved incapable of delivering on its utopian promise—has turned from living dream to living death. And it suggests that the very notion of 'rave culture' may in fact be a contradiction in terms.

Disunity

Just as the Woodstock convergence gave way to the fragmentation of seventies rock, just as punk split into factions based on disagreements about what punk was about and what was the way forward, so too has rave's E-sponsored unity inevitably refractured along class, race and regional lines. Each post-rave fragment seems to have preserved one aspect of rave culture at the expense of the others. House music, in its more song-full, hands-in-the-air, handbag form, has reverted to mere disco, the soundtrack to trad [traditional] Saturday Nite fever. Progressive house and garage is just your pre-rave metropolitan clubland coked-out élitism back in full effect.

Techno, ambient and electronica strip rave of its, well, raveyness, to fit a white studenty sensibility; it's the new progressive rock, not just because of its denegrified [synth band] Tangerine Dream textures, but because of the boys' own aura of anal-retentive connoisseurship that surrounds it, the con-

tempt for pop (i.e., handbag, any dance record that makes concessions to a 'girly' sensibility), and the vague, ill-defined conviction that something radical is at stake in this music.

Jungle also incites a similar sense of urgency and zeal, and for my money, musically substantiates it; at the same time, it's the post-rave offshoot that has most thoroughly severed itself from rave's premises. You could call it 'gangsta rave', in so far as jungle has taken on hip-hop and ragga's ethos of masked self-containment and controlled dance moves, and shed rave's abandonment and demonstrativeness (ultimately derived from gay disco). Ecstasy has been largely displaced within the jungle scene in favour of cocaine and marijuana; the latter, with its increasingly high THC content, creates a sensory intensification without euphoria, tinged with nerve-jangling paranoia. This drug-state fits perfectly jungle's ultra-vivid synaesthetic textures, hyperspatialized mix-scapes and tension-but-no-release rhythms.

Music designed expressly for the E experience is still big: the old skool rave spirit endures in Scotland, and through the

Feelings Induced by Ecstasy

Mary Bellis, an inventor and guide to inventions at About. com, describes the psychological effects of ecstasy.

[Ecstasy] is a mood/mind altering drug and like Prozac works by affecting the chemical level of Serotonin in our brains, a 'neurotransmitter' naturally present in the brain which can alter our emotions. . . . Chemically the drug is amphetamine like, but psychologically it's what's known as an empathogen-entactogen; empathogenic means the ability to communicate things to others or the ability to feel empathy towards others, and entactogenic means feeling well or good with yourself and the world.

Mary Bellis, "The Invention of MDMA or Ecstasy," About.com, http://inventors.about.com/library/weekly/aa980311.htm.

popularity of happy hardcore pretty much everywhere in Britain apart from London. Scottish bouncy techno and happy-core (aka 4-beat) have preserved in miniature form the lost euphoria and togetherness of 1988–92, but on an aesthetic level they've arrested the music's development, expunging all post-1992 developments and focusing on cheesy piano riffs, [hardcore techno DJ] Joey Beltram–style 'Mentasm' synth-stabs, shrieking diva-vocals and above all the stomping 4-to-the-floor beat (i.e., all the whiter-than-white elements that activate and accentuate the E-rush and encourage dancers to 'go mental'). Even as it resurges, happy hardcore is itself splitting up and hybridizing—one element looks set to merge with Dutch gabba to form a new, breakbeat-free sound that some call 'funcore', while there's even talk of 'intelligent' or 'futuristic' happy hardcore as opposed to mere crowd-pleasing fare.

Jungle, happy-core's estranged cousin, has of course already split up into at least three increasingly antagonistic subgenres. It seems that, once broken, the 'we' that each post-rave subgenre addresses can only get smaller and smaller; schisms and sectarianism proliferate *ad absurdum*.

Going Nowhere Fast

So the rave myth of transracial, cross-class unity lies in tatters. Still, there are various attributes shared by all the post-rave subscenes. And the two elements of rave culture that are most radical and 'subversive' are also what make it nihilistic and anti-humanist: namely, the intransitive nature of the rave experience, and the music's asexuality.

By 'intransitive', I mean the music and the culture's lack of objective or object ('to rave' is literally an intransitive verb); the cult of acceleration without destination, the creation of sensations without pretext or context. Rave culture has no goal beyond its own propagation. I first noticed this in 1992, when hardcore was in supernova, just before its disintegration into jungle, drum & bass, happy, etc. Rapt by the pirate radio stations, by the listeners' paged-in shouts and MCs' invocations, I was struck by both the crusading zeal and the intransitive nature of their utterances: 'rushing!', 'buzzin' hard!', 'get busy!', 'come alive!', 'let's go!', 'time to get hyper, helter-skelter', 'hardcore's firing!', even simply 'belief!!'. During the pirates'

phone-in sessions, it was like there was this feedback loop of ever-escalating exultation, switching back and forth between the station and the junglist 'massive' at home; the whole sub-culture resembled a giant mechanism designed to generate fervour without aim, a shared hallucination of being in-the-place-to-be. Massification, amplification and excitation: this alone was the pirates' *raison d'être*. At the heart of rave lies a kernel of tautology: raving is about the celebration of celebra-tion. Tautology is bliss, someone said; when rave culture's 'de-siring machine' [in the words of French philosophers Gilles Deleuze and Felix Guattari] is really crankin', when you're one of its cogs (locked into the pirate signal or plugged into the sound-system's circuitry), well, there's no feeling like it. Trou-ble is that the machine tends to wear out its human compo-nents; drugs are required to bring the nervous system up to speed; the human frame was not built to withstand the attri-tion of sensations.

There also comes the inevitable point at which rave's 'desir-ing machine' turns 'fascist' (as Deleuze and Guattari put it): when the single-mindedness turns to tunnel-vision, when get-ting high becomes getting out of it. Suddenly the clubs are full of dead souls, zombie-eyed and prematurely haggard. Instead of togetherness, sullen moats of personal space reappear; smiley-faces give way to sour expressions, bitter because they've caned it so hard that the old buzz can't be recovered. For some, any old oblivion will do; they become connoisseurs of poisons, mix 'n' matching toxins to approximate the old high.

Entering the 'Dark Side'

This moment of burn-out, when the scene crosses over into the 'dark side', seems intrinsic to any drug culture. It happened in Haight Ashbury [San Francisco] in the late sixties, when speed and STP [dimethoxy-amphetamine, a powerful hallu-cinogen] killed the luv 'n' peace vibe. It happened in the Los Angeles rave scene a few years ago, when punters shifted alle-giance from increasingly unreliable ecstasy to soul-corroding crystal meth (a vaporized form of amphetamine). It's also hap-pened to Scottish rave, with some punters taking five or more pills per session, and the rising use of sleeping pills like Tema-zepam (either to help the raver come down after a night of ex-

cess or just to get even more 'off ma heid').

Above all, it happened to UK hardcore in late 1992, when happy rave tunes gave way to 'dark side' jungle. Stripping away the squeaky voices and melodramatic strings (the fluffy 'feminine' and 'gay' elements that made 'ardkore ravey, jouissancey [from french *jouissance*; "PLEASURABLE RELEASE"]), DJ/producers created minimalist drum & bass, the voodoo sound of compulsion for compulsion's sake. Thematically and texturally, hardcore began to be haunted by a collective apprehension that 'we've gone too far'. At first there were tracks that exuded a vibe of dangerously overwhelming bliss, such as the jouissance-overdose title and languishing languor of 4 Horsemen of the Apocalypse's 'Drowning in her'. Then came 'dark side', a style that appeared to reflect long-term effects of ecstasy and marijuana use: depression, paranoia, dissociation, creepy sensations of the uncanny. Tunes like DJ Hype's 'Weird energy', Origin Unknown's 'Valley of the shadows' (with its 'felt that I was in a long, dark tunnel' soundbite), and an entire mini-genre of panic-attack songs like Remarc's 'Ricky', Johnny Jungle's 'Johnny' and Subnation's 'Scottie' (the latter featuring the cheerful sample-hook—'we're not gonna die, we're gonna get out of here'!).

Drug-Fueled Emptiness

The 'dark' trend was driven partly by a desire to take hardcore back underground by removing commercial, uplifting elements, thereby alienating 'lightweights'. But it also reflected the pharmacological reality of the subculture in late 1992 and early 1993: on the one hand, a dip in the quality of ecstasy, with a predominance of pills consisting of speed and LSD, or even a dash of downers or smack; on the other hand, the fact that if you take pure MDMA regularly its blissful effects wear off, leaving only the jittery speed-rush. Both syndromes (fake ecstasy 'cocktails' and tolerance of E's effects) are exacerbated because ravers inevitably take more pills in a futile attempt to recover the fast-fading rapture of the olden, golden days.

But even if you could manage to get consistently reliable high-quality ecstasy, the fact is that E-based lifestyle is a dead(ening) end; weekly use gradually empties the brain of the substances whose release MDMA triggers in a rush and gush

of euphoria. My sense is that the intransitive, go-nowhere aspects of rave culture are almost chemically programmed into MDMA itself. Among all its other effects, E incites a sort of free-floating fervour, a will-to-belief—which is why the most inane oscillator synth-riff can seem so numinously radiant with MEANING. But at the end of even the most tearing night out, there can be a disenchanting sense of futility: all that energy and idealism mobilized to no end (except to line the pockets of the promoter, and Mr Evian).

From another vantage point, rave can be seen as the ultimate postmodern experience (culture without content, without an external referent). Or as a [French author and theorist Georges] Bataille-like sacrificial cult of expenditure-without-return, a glorious waste of energy and resources into the void. Or even as the quintessence of Zen (the emptying out of meaning, via mantra [phrase repeated for meditation] and koan [riddles without answers]; the paradox of the full void). But you can have your fill of emptiness; even bliss can get boring.

Sexual Regression

There's another Zen aspect to rave music—its resemblance to tantra (Zen sex magick), which abolishes traditional sexual narrative (arousal/climax/resolution) in favour of an infinitely sustained pre-orgasmic plateau, during which the adept enters a mystic hallucinatory state. Both ecstasy and amphetamine tend to have an anti-aphrodisiac effect. E may be the 'love drug', but this refers more to *agapē* [communal, shared love] than to *eros* [erotic desire], cuddles rather than copulation, sentimentality rather than sticky secretions. E is notorious for making erection difficult and male orgasm virtually impossible. A real dick-shriveller, it also gets rid of the thinks-with-his-dick mentality, turning rave into space where girls can feel free to be friendly with strange men, even snog them, without fear of sexual consequences.

Arguably one of the few truly new and 'subversive' aspects of rave is that it's the first youth subculture that's not based around the notion that sex is transgressive. Rejecting all that old-hat sixties apparatus of libidinal liberation, and recoiling from our sex-saturated popular culture, rave instead locates *jouissance* in pre-pubescent childhood or pre-Oedipal infancy.

This was more explicit in Britain a few years ago, (when ravers sucked dummies [pacifiers], tracks sampled kiddies' TV-themes or nursery rhymes, and vocal samples were whisked up into a delirious babytalk babble), although child-like clothing, accoutrements and hair are still fashionable among American rave-girls (Bjork's space-pixie image is a big influence). It's noticeable that in the UK jungle scene—as timestretching allowed for the return of more 'mature', measured vocal passion as opposed to kartoon squeaky voices, and as coke 'n' spliff supplanted E—so too the lecherous gaze (for men) and sexy, scanty clothing (for girls) has returned.

It's intriguing that amphetamine (of whose pharmacological family E is a member) should be related to this cult of pre-sexual innocence. Speed is the anorexic drug, suppressing appetite along with sex-drive; anorexia has long been diagnosed as a refusal of adult sexual maturity and all its concomitant hassles. Speed/ecstasy doesn't negate the body, it intensifies the pleasure of physical expression while completely emptying out the sexual content of dance; it allows a 'regression' to the polymorphous 'body without organs' of infancy. Particularly for men, the drug/music interface acts to dephallicize the body and open it up to enraptured, abandoned, 'effeminate' gestures. But removing the heterosexist impulse can mean that women are rendered dispensable. As with that earlier speed-freak scene, the mods (who dressed sharp and posed to impress their mates, not to lure a mate), there's a homosocial aura to many post-rave scenes. There's a sense in which E, by feminizing the man, allows him to access *jouissance* independently rather than seek it through women. Hence the self-pleasuring, masturbatory quality to rave dance—closer to the circle jerk than the courtship rituals that most forms of dance dramatize. . . .

In Love with Nothing

The samples that feature in rave music—orgasmic whimpers and sighs, soul-diva beseechings like 'the way you make me feel', 'you light my fire', 'loving you'—induce a state of (that word again) intransitive amorousness. The ecstatic female vocals don't signify a desirable/desirous woman, but (as in gay disco) a hypergasmic rapture that the male identifies with, and aspires towards. The 'you' or 'it' in vocal samples refers not to a person,

but to a sensation. In truth, these are love-songs to the drug (or rather the synergistic interaction of drug/music/lights), love-hymns in praise of luv'd up-ness, or in the case of Baby D's 'Let me be your fantasy', a love-tribute to the rave scene/dream itself. American cultural studies professor Lawrence Grossberg (1994) cites a poll of young people in Britain which found that, while kids listen to music for three times as much of their leisure-time as kids did in the mid-1970s, they place music way down on the list of things they care about (after education, home, friends, money, sex, appearance, work, going out, sport, hobbies and football). Of their functional attitude to music (as backdrop to other more meaningful activities), Grossberg notes 'rather than dancing to the music you like, you like the music you can dance to'. All that I'd add is: 'you like the music you can drug to', the music that best intensifies the chemical's effects.

With E, the full-on raver lifestyle means literally falling in love every weekend, then (with the inevitable mid-week crash) having your heart broken. Millions of kids across Europe are still riding this emotional roller-coaster. Always looking ahead to their next tryst with E, dying to gush, addicted to love, in love with . . . nothing.

Life After Rave: The Reign of Hardcore and Drum and Bass

Chris Sharp

In the following selection music writer and frequent contributor to the *Wire* and *Spin* magazines, Chris Sharp, takes the reader on a tour of the hardcore sound that filled British dance floors with renewed energy after the collapse of the rave scene in the early 1990s. Sharp finds that hardcore's feverish breakbeats and densely layered sonic attack led directly to the flowering of creative energy in England that produced drum and bass (or "jungle," as it was popularly known), the many offspring of which continues to fuel contemporary dance music.

LOOKING BACK, THE RAVE PHENOMENON IS DIF-ficult to explain to anyone who wasn't there: You could call it an unruly union of disparate influences that proved temporarily explosive. Drugs, dance music, the libertarian spirit of the eighties, collective nostalgia for the counter-cultural engagement of the sixties, and the casual hedonism of British kids looking for a buzz—rave was an unpredictable day-glo cocktail of all this, and it transformed thousands of lives. Between 1988—the second summer of love, as it was dubbed by smiley-sporting acid house hipsters—and 1991, dance music became more than just something to dance to. It was the gateway to

■

Chris Sharp, "New States of Mind," *Modulations: A History of Electronic Music: Throbbing Words on Sound*, edited by Peter Shapiro. New York: Caipirinha Productions, in association with Distributed Art Publishers, 2000. Copyright © 2000 by Caipirinha Productions, Inc. All rights reserved. Reproduced by permission.

collective euphoria, a huge shared secret and a massive in-joke incomprehensible to the mainstream. A whole generation was in on it, meeting at motorway service stations in the dead of night to follow coded directions to illicit parties and dance until dawn. . . .

But the comedown was swift and crushing. The outbreak of outlaw spirit that spurred hundreds of thousands of people to break into warehouses and set up sound systems in remote fields was hunted down by the police and local government officials with decibel counters, bled dry by quick-buck promoters with a closer eye on their profits than on their promises, and laid open to ridicule by a string of infantile pop-rave hits like The Smart E's "Sesame's Treet" and Urban Hype's "A Trip To Trumpton." Dance music retreated back into the clubs, opting for constraint and control, and in the process created its first generation gap. Older fans, graduates of acid house clubs like Shoom in London and the Hacienda in Manchester, were happy to abandon rave's Balearic inclusiveness, to regroup in small cliques of like-minded afficionados and make their choice from the classical four-to-the-floor poise of Chicago house or the processed neo-disco of New York garage. But this movement left ravers in suburban outposts and pirate radio DJs in London's unfashionable enclaves with a thirst for speed and rhythm that the new dance establishment could not satisfy. Out of this thirst, hardcore was born.

Hardcore Rises from Rave's Ashes

During hardcore's dark ages, which lasted from the collapse of the rave adventure until jungle's charge overground in the summer of 1994, the British media had a simple, serene policy towards the music. They ignored it. Those august publications reverentially referred to as "taste-makers" by marketing types saw hardcore as a scrofulous parasite clinging to the margins of acceptability, a moody, psychotic blare consumed by zitty suburban adolescents and Ecstasy casualties with ill-mannered car stereos. They trained their spotlights instead on the tasteful, manicured pulse of "progressive house" and the smooth, metallic sheen of "intelligent techno," implying by omission that hardcore—or "'ardkore," as it was pronounced by matey initiates—was neither progressive nor intelligent.

As hindsight has triumphantly shown, this was as much a blessing as it was a mistake. Unencumbered by the demands of the critics, fuelled by the siege mentality of the true believer, and propelled into complexity by the constantly increasing power of their equipment, the 'ardkore pariahs turned their spurned and derided music into the most electrifying sound to emerge from the U.K. in thirty years. The most expressive, too. Despite its emphasis on sheer speed, hardcore came to articulate misty nostalgia, momentary rapture, urban dread, criminal moodiness, and sci-fi futurism.

Hardcore's breakneck momentum was generated by a quest for intensity—partly an attempt to recapture rave's lost Eden of MDMA bliss, partly a reflection of the flicker-frame stimulus offered by urban experience. Producers and DJs were driven by an urge to make the drums more percussive and the bass more physical than they had ever been before. Even though some desperados went to the extreme lengths of forcing open their Technics 1210 turntables and butchering the variable resistor that regulates the pitch control, Roland TR-909-generated house music running in 4/4 time at a stately 126 bpm was never going to deliver a heavy enough sound. There was only one alternative: The renegade hardcore pioneers began to experiment with the possibilities inherent in the breakbeat.

The Breakbeat

As early as 1990, proto-jungle pioneers Shut Up And Dance (a.k.a. PJ and Smiley) were using breakbeats to inject a bit of urgency into dance music. Coming out of northeast London, SUAD saw themselves as making twenty-first century hip-hop rather than house music—working with the same armory of breaks and samples, but speeding up the beats from hip-hop's standard 80–90 bpm to 126 or 130 bpm. SUAD's sound was a kind of slow-motion jungle before the fact—a celebration of urban piracy and rhythmic manipulation that existed uneasily alongside the stilted Brit-house sound of their contemporaries, but that managed to attract a huge following. Instinctively, PJ and Smiley had grasped the many advantages that breakbeats lent to dance music. Although they were limited by the equipment of the time and could only explore them in a

rudimentary way, another two or three years would see their vision explode into life.

Breakbeats have an aura of villainy. Plundered from aging slices of funk and rare groove, lifted and looped from quasi-legal *Breaks and Beats* compilations, they are of uncertain ownership, a delicious grey area. Breakbeats evoke hip-hop, plugging hardcore directly into urban experience, nodding backwards towards DJ Kool Herc and Grandmaster Flash, giving the music an unshakable, grainy immediacy. Breakbeats mean syncopation—chinks of fraught silence that keep space and tension in the rhythms, even at high speeds.

Between 1992 and 1994, breakbeats were outcasts—they had carried The Prodigy, SL2, Altern 8, and Shades of Rhythm onto the charts on the back of the huge rave fan base, and the new "progressive" dance music shrank from them in visceral disgust. Clinging to breakbeats through that time was a gesture of defiance, a statement of intent and an invigorating and obnoxious "F— you" to the mainstream house crowd to boot. . . .

Drum and Bass Evolve

But hardcore progressed with dizzying rapidity. 1993 was the crucial year, as the music's hyperactive, cartoony garishness was focused down into a succession of precision-tooled explorations. During that time, the music held the DNA for practically every future variation in fertile suspension—five or six years later, the lines of inquiry that started then [were] still being worked out in drum and bass' multiple, schismatic fragmentations.

At the time, the dominant force was the dark sound typified by Dollis Hill's Reinforced label. The music mirrored the degeneration of the rave dream, celebratory ecstasy rushes rendered queasy and menacing by overload and adulteration. The late-eighties/early-nineties Belgian sound of Joey Beltram, T99, and CJ Bolland was revisited at delirious, choppy hyperspeed. 4 Hero documented this shift in their epochal "Journey from the Light," which took the moody sparseness of their earlier 'ardkore smash "Mr Kirk's Nightmare" into ramshackle hyperspace, subjecting lush string sounds to distorting G-forces and stabbing, bleak, nameless squirms and squiggles into the heart of the mix. Nebula II's "X-Plore H-Core" went further

into de-tuned psychosis, writhing ectoplasmically around a bastardized snatch of the Wizard Of Oz, and arriving at a Teutonic climax that hammered mercilessly away at a clammy synthesized orchestral stab. Doc Scott reveled in this murky playground. Recording as Nasty Habits (a celebration of pariahdom if ever there was one), his "Dark Angel" and "Here Comes the Drumz" were the apotheosis of the dark sound—bone-chilling funk shot through with viral smears of noise.

All of which might sound pretty unappealing to the uninitiated—but the hardcore-as-horror-movie vibe managed to articulate moods and sensations that had remained voiceless. At the very least, it was a way of working the poison of the rave comedown out of the music-generating system—and at best it was an utterly compelling affirmation of hardcore's identification with the new urban underclass of post-Thatcherite Britain [the era following the administration of British prime minister Margaret Thatcher 1979–1990]. Like hip-hop in the States, dark hardcore reveled in its status as a product of its environment: The joyless inner cities of the late-twentieth century have a physical presence in the sound.

Using noises from video games and video nasties was a way of celebrating the cheap, unreflective, pirated pleasures of suburban life while simultaneously evoking the sheer moodiness of the decaying, crime-ridden inner cities in the rolling bass and hypertense, metallic percussion. The sheer delight with which the dark sound plundered these defiantly lowbrow sources deepened the scorn of the house and garage hegemony. This despite the fact that these sounds are exactly what enabled it to evoke the ultimate suburban, late-capitalist paradox of transient thrills and casual misery. Hyper-On Experience's "Lords of the Null Lines" took its "f—-ing voodoo magic" sample from the sub-[Arnold] Schwarzenegger gorefest *Predator 2*, but added a knowing glance at the essential hollowness of this kind of low-rent pleasure: Halfway through its relentlessly choppy, channel-surfing undulation, a disembodied female vocal croons the single line "There's a void where there should be ecstasy," before being sucked into the music's percussive vortex. This isn't simply a drug-reference, a gripe about defective pills, or a glum admission of inviolable tolerance levels. It's a vibrant snap critique of late-twentieth-

century consumer life—a pointer to the redemptive creativity that animated even the darkest sounds and led to less oppressively monumental achievements. . . .

New Technology, New Sounds

Hardcore's graininess and garishness were largely forced on it by the limitations of the equipment with which it was made. The expense of memory and slow processors meant that sampling time was scarce, sound quality was low, and complex blending an impossibility. The advent of the [Akai] S1000 [sampler] changed the rules, and as producers got to grips with what it could do, it changed the music, too. If hardcore was a collage—a roughneck ride through a succession of intense experiential instants—drum and bass synthesized those experiences into a swathe of new texture. Armed with the S1000, drum and bass producers could suddenly become high-tech versions of the decadent hero Des Esseintes (from J.K. Huysmans' *A Rebours*), who spent hundreds of hours constructing elaborate perfumes from an enormous array of scents. [Producers and drum and bass innovators] Goldie and 4 Hero have spoken of a three-day session in the Reinforced studio during which they sampled, manipulated, and resampled, filling DAT (digital audio tape) after DAT with hours of mutant sound and creating a priceless storehouse of raw material. . . .

If [drum and bass producers such as] Goldie, Foul Play, and Omni Trio were among those who were trying to bring musicality back into drum and bass, they were trying to do it without abandoning the locomotive force of the hardcore mentality. Others, however, had more deep-rooted reservations about hardcore's almost paranoid hyperkinesis. As early as 1991, LTJ Bukem had mapped out an alternative future for breakbeat house with an EP whose title made his view of things abundantly clear—"Logical Progression."

Unlike, say, Goldie, who came to hardcore from a solid hip-hop background, Bukem was a veteran of the London's eighties rare-groove and acid jazz scenes. His music amply reflected that grounding. The three tracks on "Logical Progression" come swathed in breathy, soft-focus keyboard chords, and the slow-motion breaks patter rather than tear at the listener. The warm, jazzy piano stabs, and live vocals (which gen-

tly inquire "Do you wanna have a good time tonight?") blend good old-fashioned soul stylings with the kind of dewy-eyed romanticism that made Liquid's "Sweet Harmony" a dawn-chorus rave anthem. . . .

During 1994 Bukem gradually gathered like-minded souls around him—PFM, Sounds of Life, Studio Pressure (a.k.a. Photek), Peshay, Wax Doctor—releasing their music, playing their dub-plates [recordings stripped down to their rhythm tracks], and in the process guiding his musical, uplifting approach away from the margins—the 4 A.M. "wind-down" sets and the sparsely populated back rooms—and right into the heart of the drum and bass movement. Eventually, he started a club night in the West End of London called Speed, a night that was to be devoted entirely to what had come to be known as intelligent drum and bass". This tag—implying, of course, that any music with a trace of hardcore's streetwise energy was somehow unintelligent—did no end of casual violence to the considerable programming skills and talents of those who chose not to make their music in this way. It did, however, go some way to guaranteeing a hipster audience when events at the other end of hardcore's sound spectrum suddenly brought the music to the attention of the world at large.

Drum and Bass Blows Up

The Speed sound had plenty of coffee table appeal, but no mass following. In fact, the club was practically deserted during its first few months. The events with an enthusiastically burgeoning audience at that time took their musical cues from somewhere else entirely—ragga. Reggae had been pumping its DNA into hardcore rave since the early nineties. Tracks like Prodigy's "Out Of Space", which sampled "Chase The Devil" by Max Romeo, and SL2's "On A Ragga Tip," which looted Wayne Smith's dancehall classic "Under Mi Sleng Teng" were chartbusting hands-in-the-air anthems. And despite the advances being made in studios around the country, producers who stuck to the simple and exhilarating amalgamation of high-velocity breakbeats and strident ragga vocals knew that they had an increasingly dancefloor friendly formula. While rave had been a predominantly white movement, events in suburbs with high black populations started to attract more

and more black punters into the music. Temples of low-end sound like the Lazerdrome in Peckham and Roller Express in Edmonton offered ragga-style MCs and pumping basslines to a multiracial audience. By the time that sound came exploding out of the bass bins at the 1994 Notting Hill Carnival [music festival] the fusion universally known as jungle was well on its way overground.

The new breed of jungle fans had no interest in the producers who had kept the faith with hardcore, laboring through the dark ages to perfect their programming skills. They just loved the tracks that gave them the best buzz, and the one track that they loved above all the others that summer was "Incredible", a collaboration between Ragga MC General Levy and the youthful producer M Beat. "Incredible," was a top ten UK hit—a feat achieved by no other jungle or drum and bass release before or since. "Original Nuttah" by Shy FX and UK Apache followed it into the charts a few months later. These records, booming belligerently out of the sound systems at Notting Hill and riding roughshod over mainstream chart pop, announced to the world that jungle was massive. And when the media smells a mass movement—and a potential new audience of consumers—it leaps on board. Within a few months, hardcore dance music was thoroughly rehabilitated, the subject of broadsheet profiles and style press guides, a fully accredited cultural phenomenon. Not long after that, jungle was advertising breakfast cereal. . . .

New Textures

By 1995, the secret was out. Drum and bass was public knowledge, a fully mediated musical genre. Naturally, outsiders began to make it. Musicians who had previously been drawn to the arty end of alternative rock like Graham Sutton from Bark Psychosis and Kevin Shields from My Bloody Valentine were enticed by this new area of avant-gardist sound manipulation. Techno auteurs like Aphex Twin, Luke Vibert, and Mike Paradinas were fascinated by the new rhythmic space that the music offered. The wayward talents of these people often imbued the music with amazing new textures—Aphex Twin's "Boy/Girl," for example, is plangently emotive and rhythmically ferocious in equal measure—but some newcomers seem

to have been attracted to the music for dubious reasons. Tom Jenkinson (a.k.a. Squarepusher) is a case in point. At the forefront of the arty drill and bass micromovement, he seems concerned less with drum and bass' exhilarating sense of community than with the opportunities for virtuoso programming flashiness that it provides. The simple fact of drum and bass' velocity was appeal enough for others. . . .

For a while, drum and bass spread and mutated with viral speed, simultaneously infiltrating TV soundbeds experienced by many millions and tiny club/art spaces known to an infinitesimally rarified few. But many central figures turned a blind eye to all this extraneous activity as well as to the glittering prize of a major-label contract. While the major-label album artists were busy using their samplers to simulate real musicians in an attempt to recreate the squelchy virtuosity of [jazz musicians] Lonnie Liston-Smith or Herbie Hancock, the underground producers busied themselves with the essence of the music—making the bass more physical and the drums more percussive, questing perpetually after the intensity and the galvanic buzz that only jungle at its finest was able to deliver. For them, musical realism was irrelevant. Samplers were a way of twisting, intensifying, and generally f—-ing up sound to increase its impact. This approach ushered in the kind of advance made by Dead Dred's "Dread Bass" (Moving Shadow's fiftieth release), that introduced the new sound celebrated in its title, a wall-crawling, slurred boom of a bassline which descended to subsonic levels and was experienced as much physically as aurally. "Dread Bass" pointed to a defiantly non-"intelligent" future dedicated to the delirium provoked by rampant mutant sound. Gradually, jungle atomized its ragga influences, plugged back into the hip-hop attitude that had inspired hardcore in the first place, and terrorized the dancefloor in the form of jump up.

Jump Up and Techstep

Jump up is perhaps the most straightforward descendent of rave. Despite the constant nods across the Atlantic, its restless, skittering progression from outrageous bassline to outrageous bassline, from drug-friendly chimes to syncopated gunshots, expresses the same nervous energy, the barely contained hilar-

ity, the lurching moodswings and the sweaty-palmed creativity of the hardcore explosion. And although jump up is a harsher, more straightjacketed distillation of that mood, the exuberance of the biomass still beats warmly at its heart. Producers like DJ Hype, Pascal, DJ Zinc, Gang Related, and Aphrodite developed the intricacy of their rhythm programming without abandoning "the funk" and inflated their basslines like sex-dolls, blowing them up into huge, marauding swathes of morphing, low-end noise.

And despite its bad-boy touches and [rap group] Wu-Tang [Clan] derived menace, jump up remained provocatively physical music. Trace elements of rare groove and the slackest ragga provided the blue-touch paper for the exploding cybernetic inevitability of the rolling drums. . . .

Some took their opposition to the jazz-jungle excesses of Bukemites like Alex Reece, Aquasky, and Dave Wallace even further, locking into the extremism of the old dark sound and pushing it towards psychosis. Ed Rush, Trace, and Nico brought the world techstep, a malevolent, seething morass shaped by many hours of late-night programming and the fluttering paranoia brought on by THC-intense Skunk weed [potent marijuana]. Like the Frankfurt industrial extremists, the techsteppers reprised the warped strings and squirming Belgian hoover sound—but they managed to intensify that mood a hundred-fold. If jump up's sonic manipulation was gleeful, techstep's was compulsive as it warped, twisted, and rewired its sound sources into balefully attenuated shapes, boiling them down into a glutinous coagulation of nameless sinister noise. . . .

The Future of Drum and Bass

It could be argued that techstep marked the end of the line. Drum and bass has since retreated into the sparse, Detroit-inflected, and stiffly mechanical constructions of neurofunk. Tracks like Jonny L's "Piper," Optical's "Grey Odyssey," and Photek's "Ni Ten Ichi Ryu" are sparse, sexless, and strangely rigid, revolving around sterile two-step drum loops and monastically eschewing any kind of play, any kind of exuberance. "I like to create atmospheres and moods by making the music as unatmospheric as possible," Photek has said. "The absence of feeling kind of becomes the feeling." This new frigidity has co-

incided in London with the rise of speed garage, which blends pumping 4/4 beats with junglist basslines and sporadic bursts of rhythmic science. On any given Sunday in East London, I can tune in to twenty or thirty pirate radio stations, but only 1 or 2 are playing breakbeats. Right now, garage rules.

The story is the same in the clubs. It's an inviolable rule of nightlife that heterosexual male clubbers inevitably follow the women, and for many women speed garage's sultry kick was a blessed relief from drum and bass's relentlessly spartan moodiness. And if the fan base is evaporating, the mass market has already lost interest. . . . Predicting the future is never an easy pastime, and it's difficult to know exactly what the next stages in the development of breakbeat science will bring, but a lengthy spell back in the underground seems inevitable. In a sense, this is where we came in, and one thing is certain—whether the world is watching or not, drum and bass will continue to evolve.

The New Age of Rave

Suzanne Smalley

In response to a growing dissatisfaction with the state of rave culture, some ravers have begun an attempt to recapture the movement's early promise of communal harmony, peace, and release through unrestricted dance and sensory stimulation. One direction that this trend has taken is toward a drug- and alcohol-free rave experience that combines all-on-the-floor dance beats with political and social awareness and new-age spiritualism. In the following article *Newsweek* correspondent Suzanne Smalley describes gatherings in New York and Chicago in 2003 to illustrate how the rave experience has taken on a new, and some would say, sanitized, form.

KIM SCHMIDT GLISTENS WITH SWEAT AS SHE dances, trancelike, to the repetitive beat coming from industrial-size speakers in the corner. It's two hours past midnight in a loft in New York City's Chelsea district, and more than a hundred blissed-out twenty somethings spin with her in the half light. Down a dark hall, in the "chill out" room, others sit—eyes closed, hands clasped—looking blank. What are these people on?

Nothing, it turns out. Or rather, Schmidt and her friends are high on "New Age raves," an underground movement that blends the healthiest elements of raves—electronic music and dance marathons—with yoga, meditation and other spiritual rites. Drugs and alcohol are strictly forbidden. All the people

■

Suzanne Smalley, "The New Age of Rave," *Newsweek*, July 7, 2003. Copyright © 2003 by Newsweek, Inc. All rights reserved. Reproduced by permission.

at this event, sponsored by a group called Body Temple, are looking for a Saturday-night party where they can lose themselves without taking anything more potent than a shot of blue-algae juice. Some are urban yoga addicts looking for new ways to get a fix. Others, like Schmidt, are refugees from the rave scene who have hit bottom and climbed back up. More than a decade after raves started in New York, Los Angeles and Chicago, club goers have had enough of overdoses and hangovers. "I was a club kid who used to try to get the high with ecstasy," says Schmidt, 27, her ponytail bouncing. "Now, I get it naturally. I like being around people who are celebrating in a healthy way. And I love to dance."

Promoters are launching holistic raves all over the country, from Oregon to Chicago to Los Angeles. In San Francisco, there's a New Age rave almost every weekend. Parties are held anywhere from yoga centers to nightclubs, and people drive hundreds of miles to attend them. Once there, they dance as if their lives depended on it, and that's just the point, says Lynn Schofield Clark. After years of grim news, from Columbine to September 11 to the Iraq war, young people need new ways to celebrate. "The idea of experiencing life and a sense of community in a way that is not risking their lives is pretty appealing," says Schofield Clark, author of "From Angels to Aliens," a book about spirituality and youth. Dr. Dean Ornish, an expert on the health benefits of yoga and meditation, would put it another way. "It's a more healthful way [than drugs] to open up into the altered states of awareness which dance and music can bring you to."

In Los Angeles, a group called Ambient Groove Temple throws all-night parties—once a month: deejays spin the hard-driving electronic music you would expect to find in a nightclub. Evenings begin with yoga and meditation sessions that last up to three hours. Then, participants listen to lectures on Eastern philosophy and how to save the environment before roaming through three rooms where they can sample a smorgasbord of raw food and herbal drinks. Massage therapists offering Thai- and shiatsu-style rubs are on call to loosen dancers' muscles before they hit the floor.

The first party was in San Francisco about three years ago, but elsewhere the trend has taken off only within the past year,

and already it has moved beyond the coasts. In Chicago a crew called TranceZenDance Tribe throws similar events, also drug- and alcohol-free. After a guided meditation focused on what organizer Travis Robb calls "linking consciousness with everyone on the planet," and a sound-healing session (in which a musician on an Aboriginal instrument called a didgeridoo circles the room, playing at everyone's feet), TranceZenDance deejays crank up the music. Images of the Taj Mahal and the Pyramids, and geometric shapes flash on a wall-size screen.

Organizers range from small-time yoga-shop owners to established nightclub impresarios. Later this year, Robert Wootton, who managed the popular Irish band Hothouse Flowers for six years, will launch a club called Spirit in New York City. Spirit will occupy the same building that used to house Twilo, perhaps the world's most famous electronica and ecstasy warehouse until it was shuttered two years ago after repeated drug busts. The new club will serve alcohol, but the drug policy will be so tough that Wootton has already spent time with New York police planning security modeled after the club he now runs in Dublin. "If we catch you consuming or selling drugs, we don't just eject you, we call the police and arrest you on the spot."

Like its Irish cousin, Spirit will feature three floors—Mind, Body and Soul—and every week deejays and performers will stage a floor show based on the creation myth. "We're taking over darkness with light," says Wootton, alluding to a time when Twilo was so plagued by overdoses that management rented ambulances to sit outside, waiting for casualties. "I've watched where the rave culture went wrong," he says. "We're trying to bring it back to its pure state."

Wootton's focus on ancient rituals would make Body Temple's acolytes feel right at home. Marketed as a "tantric circus" that "creates an environment where the tribal and the mythic coexist on the cutting edge," the New York event regularly features what may be the ultimate collision of worlds: the shamanistic trance-dance ceremony. A 28-year-old "trance-dance facilitator" named Parashakti (whose bio notes that she is "descended from a long line of Jerusalem healers") leads a rite during which she encourages everyone to find his inner "power animals." The crowd listens raptly, eyes closed and in-

haling billowing clouds of incense, while repeating her chants. After the ceremony, partygoers don blindfolds to heighten their sensory perceptions while they bust a move. Parashakti surveys her domain proudly, the diamond-encrusted bindi between her eyes flashing. Beatific kids are kicking it and the organizers are counting their profits. Just saying no to drugs never looked so cool.

The Next Frontier: The Asian Underground on the Rise

Kanika Gahlaut

In the twenty-first century electronic dance music can be heard pumping from clubs in Japan, Vietnam, Israel, Iceland, and Morocco. Kanika Gahlaut's survey of the surging dance scenes in India and throughout Asia attests to the emergence of a youth-culture phenomenon that has assumed a truly transnational, global scale. Gahlaut is a contributing writer for *India Today*, one of South Asia's most widely circulated and influential weekly news publications.

EVEN AS NORAH JONES WAS THE ONLY INDIAN (well okay, half Indian) making her way up the pop charts these past few weeks [in 2002], there has been an equally hummable success story in alternative music. Midival Punditz, the Delhi-based raga-electronica band of Gaurav Raina and Tapan Raj, released its first full-length album in the US in September and became the first Indian electronic band to make it to the Billboard World Charts.

The Punditz's schedule could well belong to an international rock star: when not touring New York and San Francisco with Bill Laswell (producer for Santana and Sting) as part of the various artistes that form Tabla Beat Science, the pair have done the DJ set with Talvin Singh in gigs in Mumbai and

■

Kanika Gahlaut, "Asian Underground: Electric Entry," *India Today*, November 18, 2002, p. 66. Copyright © 2002 by Living Media India, Ltd. Reproduced by permission.

Goa; in Delhi they have, with masterful disc scratches and loops, made crowds surrender to multi-layered music manipulation at Cyber Mehfils, their floating nightclub where the venue changes but the guest list—hardcore followers of the band—follows them. Punditz's music infuses Indian elements into electronic dance music, taking forward the "Asian Underground" movement synonymous with Talvin Singh.

When juxtaposed against the international din surrounding club music, however, the Indian sensibility is still only a faint drum and bass beat. The big beat invasion came into its own in the mid-1990s. Now radio stations give the genre dedicated airplay worldwide and hoardes throng sports arenas for "massives". What to the uninitiated sounds like repetitive beats at high decibels sometimes interrupted by semi-human noises or snatches of words that step in for lyrics, is, for the globalised generation that has embraced it, a masterful synthesis of sound. Under the leadership of the DJ, it has the power to tap into a variety of "moods" in one single track.

Political boundaries are broken down when the beats take on a subtext. The UK's embracing of Asian Underground in the late 1990s came to be symbolic of multicultural New Britain. Though Talvin Singh has been seen as the principal proponent of Asian Underground so far, to say he created the genre would be incorrect. He was, as Raina points out, the face of "a simultaneous uprising in different cities by a generation of musicians who grew up on the club culture but realised that we're Indian and that our music needed to be true to us". Now it's a whole global network. If the goateed Karsh Kale is at the forefront of the Asian Underground movement in New York (his album *Realize* was seen by critics to bring "soul" to electronica), Punditz—who have played with Ustad Zakir Hussain and Ustad Sultan Khan all over the world—has emerged as a strong force in India.

"Their efforts are sincere, but to make a mark internationally Punditz will have to be supported by a financial and cultural movement for electronic dance music as a complete genre in India itself," says Whosane?, the DJ who began playing electronic dance in India 15 years ago [in 1987]. But while the club culture is not as big in India as in Europe, the US and Japan, even the cautious say the genre has become fashionable.

Till even three years ago, Goa was the raver's heaven, the Ibiza-like space in a country that otherwise balle balle-ed to bhangra and Bollywood remixes. Now, in cities like Mumbai, Bangalore and Delhi, the suit-clad MNC [Multinational Corporation] executive and the literature student in college step out at night to tune in to the various, constantly evolving and always overlapping strains of electronic dance—the fat, loud beats of speed garage, the soulful rhythm of drums and bass, the built-up frenzy of jungle and the pure energy of psychedelic trance. "I've seen a democratisation of electronic dance music," says DJ Rummy who began hosting his first "nights" in Delhi three years ago. Whosane?, who began playing under the cover of "terraces of homes away from the city", says in recent months he was "surprised to find dance music followers in places like Hyderabad, Chennai and Ahmedabad." Perhaps the most telling example is the Ganeshotsav in Mumbai this year: Whosane? and DJ Asad, in what can only be described as a techno trance Ganesh resurgence, played atop a truck and led devotees to the immersion.

A New Respectability

Earlier hosted at farmhouses for fear of being termed "seedy" and seen as merely a background score to "the sex and drug culture", the music now has corporate respectability. Pepsi, Coke, Smirnoff and Bacardi are regular sponsors. "A couple of years ago, you couldn't walk into a store and ask for trance music," says Hardy, a trance music lover/promoter in Delhi who was among the first to "out" his parties and take them to public venues—one night at the Dome, Ambassador Hotel, he got cross-dressers to work the doors for the first time in India. "Today, they have whole sections." DJs with unpronounceable names are jet-setting to and fro. The Internet becomes the musical highway and there's a rush of traffic there—DJs use MP3 to send samples of their music to clubs and radios worldwide.

Besides this electronica exchange, there has been a growth in local talent. Following the unwritten rules of the DJ culture of this genre, the laptop wielding music-makers keep to the background, restricting their movements to shuffling in the console, never allowing personality to take over the beat as it does in pop music. Yet, DJ Light, the club name for Delhi-

based Amit Seth, a psychedelic-trance deejay, DJ Pearl, currently MTV veejay Nikhil Chinnappa's girlfriend, and Whosane? are established names known even to the Page Three reader. And even as DJs Excite, Joy, Jayant, Mickey are touted as new talents, others spring from the music mixer with increasing regularity, filling the gap separating niche from mass.

But as the followers grow, there remains a dearth of space. While the music and its specific genres have pushed for and found a permanent home in clubs worldwide—Heaven in London is known for house, Matso in Amsterdam for techno and progressive and the Ministry of Sound, London, for garage—club music lovers in India, except for weekly flirtations at five-star hotels, and Fire and Ice, Mumbai, which plays techno on Tuesdays, draw a blank. With radio being in the state it is in—though private stations have for the last four months been giving the music considerable weekend airtime—it is left mainly to floating clubs like Cyber Mehfils to ensure the genre flourishes.

So will the genre's push for space and its growing followers put India on the electronica map? Channel V VJ Gaurav Kapur says any sound that will make its mark has to be Indian: "Internationally, there is so much electronic music being made that what will be noticed is what you bring to the table." Fans believe the groundwork was done in the UK, with mainstream support coming from Madonna and Talvin Singh's tracks in *The Cell*. Raina says Indian classical was an inevitability in any music where beat reigns, bringing to it the depth critics of electronica accuse it of lacking.

That Asian Underground—or "Indian Electronica" as Tapan Raj would rather it be known—is the masala of the moment on the electronica scene is obvious from in the way international deejays use Indian sounds without having learnt Indian classical music. Buddha Bar, the bestselling Ambience Lounge music, too uses rich Indian overtones. Punditz likens its work to jazz, considered underground till it became a movement. "The use of Indian elements with electronica is a genre that like all new genres fails typecasts till it forms a space of its own, as is happening now," says Raina. Is Delhi the New Orleans of the New Age?

GLOSSARY

acid: Prefix to a number of genre names (such as acid house, acid jazz, acid trance, etc.) in which the use of the Roland TB-303 Bassline synthesizer is prominent.

acid house: A variant of house music.

ambient: Environmental music that is meant to blend in with and enhance the sounds of everyday life. Ambient music does not necessarily have to be rhythmic or melodic.

battle: A hip-hop or drum and bass DJing competition in which DJs compete against each other in short sets showcasing their skills and track selection.

beat: A unit of rhythmical noise in music that can be made up of several notes or fractions of a note. The most common beats come four per bar (a 4/4 time signature).

beat juggle: A technique performed by using two records and manipulating the arrangement of the elements (drum sounds, headnotes, vocals, etc.) from both to create a new rhythmical composition.

beatmatch: The art of synchronizing and blending two separate tracks with different speeds or tempos.

big beat: A late-1990s phenomenon combining hip-hop and break beats with rock vocals and guitars.

bpm: Short for beats per minute; indicates the speed of an individual track.

break: The part of a track where the beat or main percussive elements of a song either fade out or are isolated by the removal of the melodic part of the track.

break beat: DJ/turntable-based music built primarily upon sampled disco and funk rhythm tracks; found in a wide array of electronica subgenres.

crossfader: Also called fader or x-fader; the main component of the mixer that permits fading between individual channels or playing two channels simultaneously.

dance: General name for the dance-oriented, electronic disco music of the 1990s, encompassing subgenres such as acid house, jungle, and rave.

decks: Turntables.

deep house: House music that, whether vocal or not, stays away from the pop sensibility of some mainstream house music and blends its driving 4/4 dance beat with layered synths and samples.

Detroit techno: Detroit was the birthplace of modern techno in the early 1980s. Pioneers of the soulful, minimalist Detroit sound include Juan Atkins (Cybortron, Model 500), Derrick May, and Kevin Saunderson (Inner City).

downbeat: Electronica that uses electronic instrumentation and samples but puts them to beats that are slower than house music and (usually) hip-hop influenced.

drum 'n' bass (D 'n' B): A jazzier, more listener-friendly offshoot of jungle that emerged in the early 1990s and employed jungle's sped-up break beats with a slower bassline. As it has continued to evolve, drum 'n' bass has produced a variety of subgenres, including atmospheric, intelligent drum 'n' bass, dolphin, 2 step, jump up, dark, ragga, and jazzy drum and bass.

dub techno: The name and aural aesthetic taken from 1970s Jamaican dub reggae pioneers such as King Tubby and Lee "Scratch" Perry. Dub strips out much of the song's melody, leaving behind the rhythm section and the traces of other instruments, often with extensive, layered echo effects.

electro funk: A combination of 1970s Funk and the synths and beats emerging in the fledgling hip-hop culture. Electro funk was highly influential on hip-hop, techno, and contemporary R&B.

electronica: A term used to describe the many forms of electronically created music associated with raves. Electronica relies heavily on the use of computers, synthesizers, drum machines, and sampling.

gabber (gabba): Originating in Rotterdam, Holland, gabber is a form of dance music that employs an extremely fast beat, often topping two hundred bpm.

garage: Sped-up deep house music pioneered at the Paradise Garage club in New York. Garage was an important step in the development of drum 'n' bass.

happy hardcore (HH): A form of dance music that grafts the high speeds of garage onto bubblegum pop records by mainstream pop artists.

house: Music easily identifiable by its insistent, pulsing 4/4 beat, on top of which all sorts of music and sounds are added; an outgrowth of disco.

GLOSSARY

industrial: An often harsh and abrasive form of electro rock that often uses mechanical sounds as percussive elements. The genre takes its name from Industrial Records, the label that hosted industrial pioneers Throbbing Gristle.

intelligent dance music: Though it embraces a wide stylistic range, all intelligent dance music (IDM) aims to take dance/electronic music beyond the dance floor. IDM artists use the rhythms, breaks, and synths of more mainstream artists but experiment with these sounds in order to emphasize the listening—rather than the dancing—experience.

jungle: As with many electronic dance music genres of the 1990s, jungle is a descendant of garage. It uses break beats sped up to double time in conjunction with deep electro basslines. Although often confused with drum 'n' bass, which tends to be jazzier and less aggressive, jungle has many "hardcore" subgenres and often features MCs working in the Jamaican dub/dance hall style.

MC: Master of ceremonies—an individual who speaks or raps over the music; common in hip-hop and jungle genres.

MIDI: Musical instrument digital interface; a standard for synthesized electronic music.

mixer: One of the main pieces of equipment needed to DJ. It allows two separate sound sources to be played as one, usually with the aid of the crossfader.

organic house: House music that uses layers of live (organic) instrumentation and percussion to augment the 4/4 electro house beat.

rave: Underground gathering or party to dance to electronic music—usually trance, house, or techno—played by DJs.

remix: To remake a preexisting track; also, the product of remixing. Remixing extensively samples the source track, leaving enough similarities that the reworked version is recognizable as a variation on the original.

sample: To extract material from a previously recorded source; to drop sampled material from one track into another; or an extracted phrase from another source (e.g., another record), which is added to a live or prerecorded mix to create a new sound.

sampler: An electronic device used to play preprogrammed samples.

stylus: The tiny piece of metal at the end of the tone arm that reads the grooves of the record; commonly referred to as the needle.

techno: One of the most prominent and recognizable forms of electronica (alongside house and garage). Techno grew out of the music

that migrated from Detroit to Germany and back to the United States, where it developed in early hip-hop and electro funk.

tone arm: The elongated metal arm attached at the top right-hand side of the turntable. The stylus and cartridge are attached to the end of this arm.

trance: A form of dance music that is repetitive and droning (usually building toward a climax) techno built on hypnotic, Eastern-sounding synth lines and bleeps and bloops. The wide variety of offshoots include goa, psytrance, and progressive.

trip hop: A form of dance music that layers hip-hop beats and scratching with rock, jazz, and R&B vocals.

turntable: The piece of equipment that is used to play the records; most commonly used in pairs and in conjunction with a mixer. The industry standard is the Technics 1200.

1200: The model of Technics record player that is most popular in the world for DJing. Often the turntables are simply called "1200s."

UK garage: The London sound that emerged around 1997, when London DJs altered the New York garage sound with cavernous, half-tempo basslines.

FOR FURTHER RESEARCH

Books

Frank Broughton and Bill Brewster, *How to DJ Right: The Art and Science of Playing Records.* New York: Grove, 2003.
> For those interested in learning the basic skills and techniques necessary to be a club DJ, Broughton and Brewster, DJs and authors of *Last Night a DJ Saved My Life*, provide an indispensable guidebook that covers everything from beat mixing to sampling to the essential tricks of "turntablism."

Matthew Collin, *Altered State: The Story of Ecstasy Culture and Acid House.* London: Serpent's Tail, 1998.
> First published in 1997, *Altered State* has become something of a classic in the literature on ecstasy and house music. Collin examines the scientific history of the synthesis of ecstasy, the social history of its proliferation as a club drug, its sensationalized reception in the mass media, and its continued influence on rave and dance lifestyles.

Bruce Gerrish, *Remix: The Electronic Music Explosion.* Vallejo, CA: ArtistPro, 2001. http://artistpro.com.
> With its focus on the art of the remix, Bruce Gerrish's text guides the reader through the history of remixed music as well as the techniques and tools of the trade that any remixer needs to know. Of particular interest is Gerrish's thorough exploration of the cultural significance of MP3s, underground radio, and information technologies—developments that account for the intimate relationship between remixing and the Internet. The book's historical and instructional sections are generously interspersed with interviews with many of the most renowned contemporary DJs and producers.

Julie Holland, *Ecstasy: The Complete Guide: A Comprehensive Look at the Risks and Benefits of MDMA.* Rochester, VT: Park Street, 2001.
> An attending psychiatrist at Bellevue Hospital in New York, Julie Holland, presents a clear and objective medical analysis of all currently available research on the effects of MDMA on the human mind and body. Holland acknowledges the potential risks associ-

ated with abuse of ecstasy and considers the potential clinical benefits of MDMA in psychotherapy.

Ben Kettlewell, *Electronic Music Pioneers*. Vallejo, CA: Artist-Pro, 2002. http://artistpro.com.

This in-depth exploration of the musical revolutionaries and technological developments that spurred on the historical evolution of electronic music manages to be both comprehensively researched and entertaining. Kettlewell, a music journalist and composer in his own right, demonstrates a breadth of knowledge that allows him to range with equal expertise across subjects as diverse (yet ultimately interconnected) as the history of the theremin, German techno, laptop electronica, and gangsta rap.

Cynthia R. Knowles, *Up All Night: A Closer Look at Club Drugs and Rave Culture*. Melbourne, Australia: Red House, 2001.

Knowles offers a thorough and evenhanded examination of a wide range of illegal substances including MDMA, oxycontin, ketamine, rohypnol, inhalants, and many more that often find their way onto dance floors.

Tara McCall, *This Is Not a Rave: In the Shadow of a Subculture*. New York: Thunder's Mouth, 2002.

Tracing rave's storied development across the world from Detroit to Ibiza to London, Tara McCall takes the reader on a highly personal trek through the past and present of the rave scene. McCall takes particular care to try to render the texture and sensation of rave by bringing together vibrant photography and firsthand accounts from young ravers, many of whom are all too aware of how rave has changed over the years.

Kurt B. Reighley, *Looking for the Perfect Beat: The Art and Culture of the DJ*. New York: Pocket Books, 2000.

Kurt Reighley, editor at large for *CMJ New Music Monthly*, is also known by the DJ nickname DJ El Toro. Reighley brings his personal experience—gathered behind both the DJ's decks and the music journalist's desk—to bear on DJ culture. *Looking for the Perfect Beat* is more than just an explanation of DJ history and techniques; it is an engaging and vigorously written account of how DJs have influenced popular culture by fundamentally transforming the way music is produced, played, and consumed.

Curtis Roads, *Microsound*. Cambridge, MA: MIT Press, 2002.

At the far edge of experimental electronic music lies the theory and practice of microsound, the music world's analog to atomic

physics and genetic engineering. As Roads explains, microsound (sound particles less than one-tenth of a second in duration) involves the computer-assisted fragmentation of notes—the most basic units of recognizable sound—into minute sound components that can then be manipulated, combined with fragments from other notes, and built into previously inconceivable sound structures. Roads's analysis is well researched and informed by musical theory but remains accessible to the uninitiated reader.

Peter Shapiro, ed., *Modulations: A History of Electronic Music: Throbbing Words on Sound.* New York: Caipirinha, 2000.
　　A tie-in to filmmaker Iara Lee's documentary of the same name, *Modulations* is a visually innovative tour through many of the subgenres that comprise contemporary electronic music, including from acid house and techno to hip-hop, ambient, and drum and bass. This anthology gathers together contributions from renowned music writers, including Simon Reynolds, Tony Marcus, Peter Shapiro, and Kurt Reighley, along with interviews with key composers and performers.

Dan Sicko, *Techno Rebels: The Renegades of Electronic Funk.* New York: Billboard, 1999.
　　Tracing the emergence of techno music as one of the most significant popular musical forms of the late twentieth century, Dan Sicko begins with the American techno explosion of 1997–1998 and then moves back in time to techno's roots in 1970s' funk. On the way back to premillennium America, Sicko—a music writer for publications such as *Rolling Stone, Urb*, and *Wired*—stops off in the UK, Detroit, Chicago, and New York as techno undergoes its key transformations and becomes a global phenomenon. The book ends with a speculative look toward the future of techno music and an informative discography and buyer's guide for those interested in familiarizing themselves with seminal techno recordings.

Mireille Silcott, *Rave America: New School Dancescapes.* Toronto, ON: ECW, 1999.
　　Mireille Silcott, the coauthor of *E: A Book About Ecstasy* and the former music editor of the *Montreal Mirror*, charts rave's American emergence from the club culture of the 1970s and 1980s and into the whirlwind years of the 1990s. In lucid and accessible prose that invites both scholarly and general readership, Scott examines the many different regional types of rave and the particular forms of community that each fostered. Particular attention is paid to the relationship between rave and cross-country gay circuit parties,

which makes a valuable contribution to the reader's comprehension of rave's cultural significance.

Sarah Thornton, *Club Cultures: Music, Media, and Subcultural Capital.* Hanover, CT: Wesleyan University Press, 1996.
Sarah Thornton, lecturer in media studies at the University of Sussex, England, takes a scholarly and theoretically informed look at club cultures (Thornton applies the post-Marxist theories of French sociologist Pierre Bourdieu) and how alternative categories of taste and the elusive quality of "cool"—or "subcultural capital," as Thornton terms it—offer adherents of marginal cultural movements an identity outside of the mainstream. Thornton makes a particularly valuable contribution to the analysis of club culture with her work on the gendered sociological and cultural meanings of clubbing and dance music for women.

David Toop, *Ocean of Sound.* London: Serpent's Tail, 2001.
Renowned composer and music writer Toop's unique book is a combination of history, musicology, philosophy, and metaphysical meditation on ambient music and the beauty and power of electronic composition. Toop intersperses his ruminations with probing interviews with artists as diverse as Sun Ra, Brian Wilson, Aphex Twin, and Brian Eno.

Frank Trocco and Trevor Pinch, *Analog Days: The Invention and Impact of the Moog Synthesizer.* Cambridge, MA: Harvard University Press, 2002.
Although the history of electronic music has been told many times, this account of the early days of the analog synthesizer (from the mid-1960s through the mid-1970s) offers a unique lens on the musical, sociological, and even economic impact of synthesizer technologies on popular culture. Although Trocco and Pinch place Robert Moog (inventor of the Moog analog synthesizer, which revolutionized pop and rock music) at the front and center of this cultural history, they also offer informative investigations of the technologies of competing inventors, as well as the contribution of rock/pop composers that helped to popularize the once utterly radical synthesized sound.

Tony Verderosa, *The Techno Primer: The Essential Reference for Loop-Based Music Styles.* Milwaukee: Hal Leonard, 2002.
Composer Tony Verderosa (or VFX, his DJ pseudonym) infuses this hybrid history and instructional text with a vivid enthusiasm for computer-based music befitting the New York–based per-

former and producer. The book and accompanying CD, packed with profiles of key figures in electronic music history and interviews with many of today's leading electronica artists, entertains, informs, and guides the inexperienced composer through the basic techniques for programming loops and constructing songs.

The Rough Guides Series

The Rough Guides series provides some of the most comprehensive surveys of contemporary musical genres, covering essential recordings and providing informative biographies and commentary with an attitude. Readers of *Examining Popular Culture: DJ, Dance, and Rave Culture* who are interested in further investigation into some of electronic music's most enduring subgenres will be interested in the following volumes:

Tim Barr, *The Rough Guide to Techno*. London: Rough Guides, 2000.

Sean Bidder, *The Rough Guide to House Music*. London: Rough Guides, 1999.

Peter Shapiro, *The Rough Guide to Drum 'n' Bass*. London: Rough Guides, 1999.

Web Sites

The Bomp Bookshelf, www.bomp.com/BompbooksTechno.html#MBTS.
> This site, operated by the Bomp! Independent record label and mail order service in Burbank, California, offers a comprehensive catalog of hard-to-find books about rave, DJ culture, and electronic music. Links to other areas of Bomp's site will bring Web surfers to listings of recordings and publications on a broad range of underground music.

The Cortical Foundation, www.cortical.org.
> Founded by Gary Todd in 1992, the Cortical Foundation is dedicated to the preservation of sound archives and publication of recordings, with particular emphasis on electronic artists that emerged during the 1960s.

DJ Forums, www.djforums.com.
> This site's bold slogan, "the center of electronic music culture," is

well earned: Whether your interest is hip-hop, house, drum and bass, or anything that requires turntables, DJ Forums is an indispensable hub for electronic music–related information on the Web. Forums for members and guests are at the heart of this massive site that also includes articles, record and equipment reviews, tutorials on DJ and mix techniques, an event guide, and Faderwave radio, a continuous mix of music by DJ Forums' members.

DJ History.com, www.djhistory.com.

DJs Bill Brewster and Frank Broughton, authors of *Last Night a DJ Saved My Life* and *How to DJ Right*, operate this Web site for professional DJs, aspiring spinners, and curious onlookers. This site's extensive offerings include feature articles and interviews with major stars, a forum for the exchange of questions and opinions, a UK record shop guide, MP3s of DJ mixes, Brewster's and Broughton's personal sites, and many useful links.

Electronic Music Interactive, http://nmc.uoregon.edu/emi.

The New Media Center at the University of Oregon maintains this unique site, a multimedia primer that introduces the basic vocabulary and concepts of electronic music theory and composition. Users navigate the innovative and easy-to-use point-and-click interface to watch and listen to Shockwave presentations that clarify key terms and essential techniques.

Electronic Music World, www.electronicmusicworld.com.

An electronic music 'zine devoted to all things electronica. Packed with music reviews, feature articles, links to independent labels and music downloads, Electronic Music World also boasts a BBS divided into a wide variety of categories for discussion communities interested in anything from technology to recordings to the dance and rave lifestyle.

Karlheinz Stockhausen, www.stockhausen.org.

Stockhausen's personal Web site is a treasure trove of information, music, and concepts. Although the site is obviously dedicated to Stockhausen's work and ideas, it also offers a great deal of information on electronic composition in general.

Ohm: The Early Gurus of Electronic Music, www.furious.com /perfect/ohm.

In 2000 Jason Gross and Thomas Ziegler released *Ohm: The Early Gurus of Electronic Music 1948–80*, a three-CD compilation of seminal recordings from the history of electronic music. This site, hosted by Gross's long-running online music magazine *Perfect*

Sound Forever (www.perfectsoundforever.com), offers memoirs by and interviews with key figures in the development of electronic music as well as essays on historically significant recordings and composers by such music-world luminaries as Thurston Moore, DJ Spooky, and David Toop, among many others.

Rave Culture, www.cbel.com/rave_culture.

Dedicated to tracking rave-related activity in North America (including Canada) and the United Kingdom, Rave Culture categorizes 240 individual sites by region and topic, allowing users to locate rave events and dance-culture communities in their area.

INDEX

ERVIN TRASK MEM. LIBRARY
PLAINVILLE HIGH SCHOOL

P9-EMR-534

DATE DUE

FOLLETT

ERVIN TRASK MEM. LIBRARY
PLAINVILLE HIGH SCHOOL